Real Estate Investing

Create Passive Income through Rental Property Management. Choose the Right Location and Learn Successful Strategies to Buy, Rehab and Resell to Maximize Your Profits

Andrew Bennett

© **Copyright 2020 - All rights reserved.**

The content contained within this book may not be reproduced, duplicated or transmitted without direct written permission from the author or the publisher.

Under no circumstances will any blame or legal responsibility be held against the publisher, or author, for any damages, reparation, or monetary loss due to the information contained within this book, either directly or indirectly.

Legal Notice:

This book is copyright protected. It is only for personal use. You cannot amend, distribute, sell, use, quote or paraphrase any part, or the content within this book, without the consent of the author or publisher.

Disclaimer Notice:

Please note the information contained within this document is for educational and entertainment purposes only. All effort has been executed to present accurate, up to date, reliable, complete information. No warranties of any kind are declared or implied. Readers acknowledge that the author is not engaging in the rendering of legal, financial, medical or professional advice. The content within this book has been derived from various sources. Please consult a licensed professional before attempting any techniques outlined in this book.

By reading this document, the reader agrees that under no circumstances is the author responsible for any losses, direct or indirect, that are incurred as a result of the use of information contained within this document, including, but not limited to, errors, omissions, or inaccuracies.

TABLE OF CONTENTS

Introduction 8

    What are Rental Properties? 9

    Residential Rental Properties   10

    Commercial Real Estate   12

    Pros and Cons of Rental Properties 13

Chapter 1 Understanding Property Management 16

    What is Rental Property Management?   16

    Knowing the Types of Real Estate Owners   17

    Maintaining the Property   19

    Understanding Good Management 19

    Knowing that you are the Best Manager   23

    Knowing your Strengths and Weaknesses   23

Chapter 2 Real Estate Investments 26

The Many Benefits Of Real Estate 28

Chapter 3 The Art of Closing The Deal 37

Consider Using A Closing Agent 38

Make Use Of A Quiet Title 39

Hire Your Own Maintenance 40

Don't Get Sued! 41

Take Environmental Stock Of Your Property 41

Learn To Trust Your Gut 42

Chapter 4 Potential Risks 44

Safety 44

   Managing Strangers 45

   Communicate on the Main Airbnb Site   46

Competition Is Fierce 48

Bad Tenants 49

Legal Problems 51

Risk Of Vacancy 52

Chapter 5 Location Research 54

Market Research 57

   Identify Your Competition   58

   Understanding Listings   59

Best And Worst U.S. Cities For Airbnb 61

   Best Places for One- and Two-Bedroom Properties   62

   Worst Places for One Bedroom Properties   63

   Worst Place for Two Bedroom Properties. 63

Chapter 6 Analyzing A Rental Property 65

Chapter 7 Getting Funds Needed for Wholesaling 81

Chapter 8 Finding Property That Is Prime for Flipping 98

Chapter 9 Real Estate Investment Deals 112

Chapter 10 Buying Your Property 131

Chapter 11 Finding Pre-Foreclosure Properties 144

Chapter 12 The Bold Offer 150

   The How 151

      Private Sellers 151

      Agents 152

   What You Should Know When Making Your Offer 153

   Your Earnest Money Deposit 155

      How much do you have to deposit?   156

      Who should keep your earnest money deposit? 157

      What happens to your earnest money deposit? 157

   Secrets Of Successful Offers 159

   The Offered Price 160

      Time and Market   161

Chapter 13 How To Find Real Estate Investment Properties? 163

Conclusion 178

Introduction

Real estate is a progressive and attractive industry. The real estate market, which today represents a multi-billion-dollar market, continues to grow and is an integral part of life. In short, we are all aware of the need to have a roof over our heads, whether at home, at work, at our leisure activities, etc., and these roofs are built with certain materials and for a specific purpose. The main factors in understanding the structure of real estate are expressed in the following concepts: economy, risk, and investment.

Conceptually, real estate investing is simple. The goal is to invest money to increase it; thus, in the future, even more, the money will be available. Although all investments involve a degree of risk, the potential profit must cover the amount of risk involved. For example, consider the game of monopoly. To win, you buy properties, you avoid bankruptcy, and you rent to buy even more properties. If only it was that simple! In life, the concept is quite similar, but an error in your investment process can have serious consequences.

We have developed this guide to guide and guide you through the basics of real estate investing and help you make the right choices so that you can capitalize on real estate investing for a financially healthy future. Although this guide is not complete, it will provide you with a basic understanding to assist you in getting started from a professional and personal point of view.

Investing in rental properties is a very lucrative business, as these properties can generate wealth. But you need to be prepared for what it takes to own rental properties. Owning rental properties can have some financial benefits but can also have certain drawbacks such as lack of liquidity, the potential for difficult tenants, and the cost of management.

There are great risks involved in delving into something you know little or nothing about. Knowing the risks involved and how to manage rental properties will keep you off any damages that can happen in the future. Therefore, this book will serve as a guide for managing your rental properties.

What are Rental Properties?

A rental property is a type of property in which the owner receives payment for renting out such property.

For instance, a landlord receives payment for renting out his house; this payment serves as returns for renting out his property. Rental properties can be for residential or commercial purposes. Examples of rental properties are real estate for housing purposes, storage spaces, lands, etc.

Rental properties are meant for renting or leasing. Renting is an agreement backed up with an amount of money for the temporary utilization of a property that is owned by another. Residential rental properties can only be used for residential purposes, while commercial rental properties are leased or rented to carry out commercial activities.

Residential Rental Properties

Residential rental properties are properties purchased by investors and are strictly for residential purposes. These properties are inhabited by tenants based on a rental agreement. This type of property is meant for dwelling.

Residential properties can be townhouses, single-family homes, condominium units, duplexes, and the likes. There are lots of tax advantages that come with owning residential rental properties. Owning residential rental property is a very lucrative business as shelter is a very basic need.

This type of rental property offers long-term appreciation, tax benefits, monthly cash flow, and leverage using borrowed money. Although there are some risks associated with owning residential rental properties, mismanagement of these properties could be one great disadvantage of investing in residential rental properties.

Types of Residential Rental Properties

There are different types of real estate available for rent. These rental properties are categorized based on their size and the features they offer.

Single-family house: Most rental property owners start with a single-family house or townhome. These types of rental properties are very easy to own and manage. It is best for landlords who are new in the real estate industry; such landlords will be able to gain the experience and skills required for managing a rental property.

Duplexes and subdivided houses: This category of real estate includes houses having 2 to 4 units. Real estate owners that plan to dwell in one of the units themselves often prefer these types of properties.

Small multi-family buildings: These types of real estate always have about 30 units, and they are best managed with on-site management.

Large multi-family apartment building: These are rental properties that have 30 or more units in just one location with maintenance staff. Owning this type of real estate is the major goal for many rental property owners who look forward to hiring a professional property manager.

Commercial Real Estate

Commercial real estate is a type of property simply used for business purposes. This type of property is exclusively for commercial purposes. Commercial real estate ranges from a big shopping mall to a gas station. Other examples of commercial real estate are hotels, restaurants, office space, strip malls, hospitals, and the likes.

The two major categories of rental property are commercial real estate and residential real estate. There are four major classes of commercial real estate; they include industrial, office, retail, and multifamily. Commercial real estate requires more funds than residential real estate. The duration of commercial leases can range from a year to 10 years.

Commercial real estate has lots of benefits, which include capital appreciation, a high source of income, stable flow of cash from long-term tenants, and hedge against the stock market. Although there are lots of benefits, investing in commercial real estate has some disadvantages like an illiquid asset, greater regulation, requires more capital, and higher costs in renovating.

Pros and Cons of Rental Properties

Investing in rental properties has benefits and disadvantages. You need to know the pros and cons of rental properties before choosing to invest in them.

Pros:

Tax benefits

There are lots of tax benefits you get from rental properties. Rental property owners are allowed to deduct expenses like maintenance costs, damages, and insurance interests. The "2017 Tax Cuts and Jobs Act" offers some new tax benefits for landlords.

Meeting different people

Owning a rental property offers you the benefit of meeting different people. If you are someone that likes meeting people, owning a rental property is a great opportunity to interact with all types of people.

Stable income flow

Rental properties allow you to have a stable flow of income. Rents will always have a due date, and owning a rental property simply means a stable income flow.

1031 Exchange

The '1031 Exchange' simply implies that a rental property can be sold, and you can invest in another king of that business without having to pay capital gains taxes.

Cons:

The rise in insurance premiums and taxes

Your mortgage's interest and the principal may be fixed, but this does not mean that taxes will remain stable. Insurance premiums can also increase with time.

Lack of liquidity

Rental properties are not a liquid asset. It can take several months to get a tenant. And if you need the money urgently, you might not be able to get the best price.

Difficult tenants

This is one of the most challenging problems you might have to deal with. If you own a rental property, you need to prepare yourself for confrontational and adversarial relationships with people. For instance, you can end up having tenants that are disobedient and destructive. You need the patience to deal with tenants like this.

Maintenance

A property owned needs to be taken care of. As a rental property owner, you will need to take care of major and minor damages. A property that is not maintained will easily wear out and get damaged; it is, therefore, necessary to keep your property in good condition.

Chapter 1 Understanding Property Management

A property needs to be well taken care of so that it can be in good condition. When we talk about property management, we simply mean overseeing commercial and residential estate to maintain the good condition of this estate. Property management involves managing a property owned by another entity. A property manager ensures that the value of a property is preserved while income is being generated.

What is Rental Property Management?

Some rental property owners do not even know what it takes to manage a property. There are several aspects of managing rental properties; they include recording income and expenses, maintaining your property, and managing people. The most difficult aspect of rental property management is managing people.

Managing your rental property requires you to have interactions with many types of people. Apart from your tenants, you will have interactions with contractors, government employees, rental prospects, and suppliers. Managing people is the most challenging aspect of property management.

The ability to interact with people and create healthy relationships with them is the most important skill required to be a successful property manager. If you are someone that likes interacting with other people and love working with people, then you can start well as a successful property manager.

Knowing the Types of Real Estate Owners

Rental property management has existed for so many years since property owners realized the income they could generate from renting or leasing their buildings or land to tenants. These days, people own properties in different ways. Property managers need to know the different types of real estate owners. There are two categories of real estate owners, and they are:

The long-term investment real estate owner

The value of the real estate has been increasing for the past decade. Many people have found out that investing in real estate is very lucrative. Owning real estate does not come easy; many people work for years to own a house and then get to know the benefit of owning a rental property.

Today, people prefer to supplement their retirement plans with extra sources of income and owning real estate has been considered as one of the wealth-builders of our time. People find out that having a stable flow of income without having to work all through your lifetime is very appealing. Even people having white-collar jobs have a limited income, which is based on how often they work. These people do have limitations in the way they earn money.

The long-term investment allows you to generate more income throughout your entire life than you can generate with only one source of income. Investing in real estate provides you with an additional flow of income. Real estate investment provides one of the best ways to generate a steady flow of income regardless of whatever you are doing; either you are sleeping, eating, or enjoying yourself.

The inadvertent real estate owner

Some property owners find themselves in the real estate business by mistake; they never planned to be a real estate owner. Many real estate owners started their rental property business through unforeseen circumstances. These are a few examples:

• You have a duplex where you found out you can live in one unit and rent out the other unit.

- You migrated to another place but couldn't sell your home, so you rented out the property because you felt it would be a great additional source of income.
- You inherited a house from your parents, and you do not want it to be abandoned.

Maintaining the Property

When you own something, you need to maintain it so that it would remain in good condition. When you own just a few units, or you just started the rental property business, you might feel you can do the maintenance work yourself. But when you start acquiring more properties, you realize you need to employ a property manager.

If you have more rental properties, you will need to employ someone that will be responsible for the management of your properties. You will also need to work with competent suppliers and vendors. You have to know that what you pay for is what you get. The cost of maintaining a property can be one of the greatest expenses in property management.

Understanding Good Management

You need to know about good management. Good management simply has a rental property that is well maintained and inhabited by paying tenants that treat the property as their own. Management is not as easy as we think; therefore, a rental property owner must understand what it takes to be a good manager.

Good management yields positive financial results. The key to being a successful rental property owner is having good tenants that stay for several years, obey all rules, pay their rents when due, and treat the property well. It is much easier to state the characteristics of a good tenant than finding one. One of the most challenging aspects of property management is managing and dealing with tenants.

Bad management can affect your rental property investment negatively. If you have a bad tenant or you do not address maintenance issues, your rental property may turn into a nightmare. A newbie in rental property investment can realize that the investment is turning into a pit. It is good you learn what rental property management is all about before investing in it.

Time management

Knowing how to manage your time is a very important aspect of rental property management. Most real estate owners see their rental unit management as a part-time job. Managing your time is all about evaluating the amount of time you have and then streamlining your tasks in line with the amount of time you have and thereby maximizing that time to yield a good result.

Managing rental property might be a part-time job, but this job requires a lot of patience, hard work, consistency, and time. Most people always assume they have what it takes to manage any property issues until they find out that managing real property is another ball game entirely. As a rental property owner, you might find it interesting to manage your property and also enjoy the cost savings. When you start acquiring more properties, you will realize that you need more time to manage your properties.

Delegating management activities

As a rental property owner, you may have lots of tasks to accomplish. However, you can choose to accomplish some tasks yourself and delegate some to others; this will make work easier for you. There are ways you can delegate some management tasks and responsibilities to some professionals. These professionals are:

A maintenance expert: As a rental property owner, you will need maintenance professionals. You need to understand that the task of a property manager is quite different from a maintenance expert. You can hire a maintenance expert that will help you handle the maintenance of your property.

A property manager: A property manager ensures your property is in good condition while it is leased out to tenants for an agreed price. You can delegate a large percentage of the tasks to a professional property manager.

An accountant: Some property owners may not have the discipline required to keep good track of income and expenses. Property owners should have an accountant that will help you in keeping good records of income generated and expenses incurred.

A rental locator service: Some real estate owners employ the services of a rental locator to offer prescreened rental applicants.

A legal expert: Owning a rental property comes with a lot of responsibilities, including legal ones. As a property owner, you might find yourself having a legal issue with one of your tenants, and this will require you employing a landlord-tenant attorney. However, you do not need to wait to have legal issues before you employ a landlord-tenant attorney.

Knowing that you are the Best Manager

You have to know that no one will manage your real estate as you will. No matter who you employ to help you oversee your property, you are still the best manager. You have more zeal to manage your property than anyone else does. This is because you are the only one that knows what it takes to own real estate, you know the stress, the sleepless nights, and efforts you made to own real estate.

Knowing your Strengths and Weaknesses

Managing a rental property requires experience and skills; you need to know that you are not managing just anything; it is a real estate. Rental property management requires you to manage people, keep records of income and expenses, and market your property. You do not need to earn a certificate before you can get started. As you get started, you will learn lots of new things.

One of the most important things you need to do before deciding to manage your property yourself is to analyze your skills and be honest with yourself. You need to know if you have what it takes, and you are ready to manage your rental property. Examine your weaknesses and strengths; know that rental property

owners must love to work with people. Ask yourself some tough questions like:
- Am I a patient and tolerant person?
- Am I well-organized in my day-to-day activities?
- Do I love working with people and having them around?
- Do I have the ability to manage my time well?
- Do I have the temperament to handle some problems, react to complaints, and render services well?
- Am I good at keeping financial records?
- Do I have sales skills?
- Do I know how to negotiate well?
- Am I willing to dedicate the time and effort to manage a property?
- Am I ready to learn more about managing a property?

If most of your answers are yes, then you should be able to manage your rental property without much difficulty. You need to answer these questions with honesty. Treat all your tenants equally and ensure you remain calm and patient under pressure. Make sure you stand firm in decision-making; do not be sentimental when it comes to decision-making. Also, ensure you maintain positive behavior.

Chapter 2 Real Estate Investments

Many people, over the last decade, in particular, have been able to increase their net worth considerably, indulge themselves in dreams and pleasures without going broke, reach and exceed financial goals and even retire as early as they wish to. Most of these became a reality for them just because they decided to look into the investment opportunities in real estate and delve into it. As we speak, real estate investment is top on the list of most worthwhile and credible routes to financial independence. And, the most incredible thing about it is that a lot of these people have achieved this with a little amount of money, or nothing at all to start with. Although the economic factors of a particular country or zone influence it's market and demand level, and it is not the path to easy riches, real estate investment defies geography and can be a useful wealth creation path for anyone irrespective of where they reside or what they do. It's 'staying power' makes it stand out from other investment options in vogue today.

Another status quo that it defies is that during economic relapse, the demand from buyers may reduce, and the packages available will always present better opportunities. So instead, those that invest in real estate at that moment have a better appreciating opportunity. At this point, it may just be safe to say that having knowledge of the market fluctuation and capitalizing on them is the secret to flourishing in real estate investments. Because people will always need to buy or lease properties, you'll never be at loss of buyers as an investor because you have the 'good' they demand.

In this chapter, we're going to examine the benefits of real estate, why the industry is in vogue in terms of investment at the moment, and the many benefits you stand to gain from indulging it.

The Many Benefits Of Real Estate

There's a pool of things you can do with your investment in real estate. While you may not realize some of them, the opportunities and benefits that come with it are unlimited. Here are some of them:

1. Great Appreciation Advantage

For more emphasis, this is usually regarded as one of the most popular and major benefits of real estate investment. Without even doing anything to your property, it characteristically appreciates by a four to five percent rate yearly. This means that you don't bother to force appreciation by renovating or improving your properties in any way. You only allow it to appreciate as the regular market grows. But you may push the appreciation rate when you put in work that makes it even more valuable than when you first acquired. So, it's possible that a family that acquired a home some ten years ago (and renovates it periodically) can find the value double or triple what they bought it for. If they give the property another ten to fifteen years, they're looking at doubling what they have at the moment in equity.

2. Profit from Equity Buildup

Having one or more properties that increase in market value over time builds your equity on them at the same time. It's a win-win situation because you get profit on your property and can divert your equity buildup as an additional investment in another area.

3. Running Your Own Business

Investment in real estate is a form of passive income/business. You still get to work on your major job, whether full time or part-time. It doesn't divert so much of your time and attention and gives you a chance for your regular business according to your goals and schedules. Not all investment and income options give this unique benefit.

4. Generating Useable Positive Cash Flow

The reason some people invest in real estate is for the sole reason of giving them out on rent to other people. That's another major benefit because it generates positive cash flow for them that can be used whenever they want. The total amount of rental fee (excluding equity buildup), more often than not, surpasses the total expenses of the entire property. You can also decide to put out your property on lease and give the lessee the option of purchasing it in the future. They're also in charge of maintaining the property for you, which is an additional advantage to the money you'll be generating from the lease periodically. Whichever way you decide to give out your property, you're still generating cash from your investment while it's still in your name.

5. Dependable Route to Making Money With Low Startup Cost

The risk of failing at a real estate investment is relatively low. Because the market is ever increasing, you can start to invest in it with little capital (more on this coming later on) and expand later on. As a matter of fact, you can start with no capital of your own. As impracticable as this may sound, you can take advantage of individuals who want to invest in real estate but don't know-how, or those who don't have the luxury of time to do so. These sets of people are looking for people to serve as intermediaries. If you have considerable knowledge of how the investment works, you can use this as a step to further your personal investment goals.

6. Multiple Channels of Profit

There are various ways through which money can be made with real estate investment. No matter your level of input, there's always something for everyone. You only have to get the hang of how the different deals and packages work and then rightly maneuver your way through them to maximize your financial goals with time.

7. Effective Anti-inflation Scheme

Not many investment options provide the kind of security this investment gives you during an economic downturn. Even during inflation, the opportunities in real estate are still guaranteed because properties are tangible and can hardly go anywhere. Real estate prices become even higher, and by chance, you have a very attractive property, you stand the test of time because of your investments.

8. Simple Marketing Strategies

Another benefit is that you don't have to pull publicity stunts and invest so much money in marketing before you put your property out there. Sometimes, all you may need is a 'For Sale' sign in front of the property you want to sell. Or in the case of rent or lease, an ad in the dailies or on social media, with the aid of your local realtor alone, can reel in prospective customers, and your property is sold in no time. It's really that simple.

9. Real Estate's Repeatability Advantage

Mastering the real estate skills is just one time. Afterward, even if you want to keep investing in different real estate, the skills you have mastered that one-time is good enough. You'll only need to adjust it to the particular type of property and adapt with the advancement in general life setting. Although you'll need to advance these skills, it's way easier than learning all over again.

10. Power Team to Achieve Goals

A successful real estate investment is in no way achievable by one man. There are various aspects that you'll need several experts to help you run. The basic services you'll need to engage are realtors or agents, tax and accounting experts, real estate lawyers, brokers, home inspectors, mortgage brokers, contractors, builders, or even architects as the case may be. Getting involved in real estate investment gives you an avenue to interact with and engage these individuals or teams from different fields. In business, generally, you will go a long way with a good network and established relationships. They may help or even partner with you in your investment, buy or at least connect you to potential customers. As the saying goes, it's who you know and not what you have that pushes you forward, sometimes.

11. Finding Investment Opportunities Easily

Just like it's easy to dispose of properties when you want to, it is the same way its acquisition works. The opportunities are everywhere you look. It only requires a little effort from you and using some of your already established relationships to get at your goal. No matter the time limit that you have, as long as you're talking to the right people and pulling the right strings, there's an investment opportunity by the corner waiting to be found.

12. Lending a Helping Hand to Others

You may already know about real estate investment being an opportunity to make money, but you may have never considered it an opportunity to help other people. Take, for instance, a bank about foreclosing a relative's house because of a debt they owe. You can use the real estate investment opportunity to save them and up your financial credits at the same time. You can also use it as an opportunity to maintain a property for someone else who's unable to do that in the meantime.

13. Tax Benefits

Using tax laws to your best advantage is one skill that cannot evade thriving in any kind of business. Consulting with tax professionals is a step in the right way. They're in the best position to tell you how to maneuver depreciation to your advantage, write off some excess expenses and take advantage of the available tax breaks.

When you invest in real estate, there are a couple of other opportunities for success, asides these aforementioned benefits, that accrue regardless of your financial situation, goals, or location. Some of them include:

1. Short and Long-term Strategies

Real estate allows you to pick investment options that suit your current needs or schedules. You can decide to engage either the short term or long term strategies. Short-term strategies allow you the option of purchasing a property a little bit below the regular market value and holding it for a very limited period of time. Within this short period, you can rehab the property and sell it as soon as you can for a quick profit. This strategy is referred to as wholesaling or quick-turning properties. A lot of investors take on this strategy to earn a lot of quick money as they need it. It isn't unusual to see individuals buy several properties in a short span of time, make a number of improvements to them, and not too long after; they sell them off at higher prices. These kinds of income are regularly used to offset debts, start a business, or just generate extra income.

A long-term strategy, on the other hand, lasts longer and can be to buy a property at fair market value or below and rent or lease it out for many years with the option of purchase. The equity you build from these rents and payments helps you decrease your current mortgage.

2. Abundant Opportunities

The area you live or invest in may determine the type of investment option you'll take on, but you'll still make money from real estate regardless. While in low-income areas, leasing and rental may be ideal because you have more opportunities to rehab your properties compared to other areas. The moderate-income areas bring along with them plenty of profits from reselling properties while combing rentals also.

3. Multiple Finance Options

There are a number of financing options that are available when you're investing in real estate. You only need to look out for them and pick the one that works best for you. You can take advantage of the opportunities that diverse government-sponsored programs bring, or can capitalize on seller financing, or just source for capital to finance your investment. You just have to know how to look for them.

Real estate provides boundless opportunities for profit in ways a lot of people may have never thought possible. The key is learning the tricks and then using them to your best advantage. Luckily, that's what this book looks to achieve.

Chapter 3 The Art of Closing The Deal

Sometimes we get so excited about a new project or development in life that we forget the most important part—closing the deal. And the same is very much true in real estate. Because whether you are dealing with tax liens, tax deeds, or investments made into platforms such as Airbnb; being able to have a concise order of operations from beginning to end is of invaluable importance. You need to see where you have been in order to know exactly where you are going.

You see, as much as we put into the beginning and opening of a deal, we need to put just as much into the closing of the deal. Don't get so giddy during the finalization process that you lose track of what you are doing, forget how to shake hands, sign papers, and make an all-around general mess of things right at the last minute! Because guess what? If you get a little lackadaisical toward closing and don't cross your t's and dot your I's like you need to; what would have been a net gain could suddenly turn into a net loss.

A prime example of this would be the scenario mentioned earlier in this book regarding folks waiting too long to make good on their tax lien certificate and going past the expiration date to claim property. This of course results in the investor having to forfeit their entire investment. They momentarily took their eye off the ball and struck out as a result. Having that said, let's take the time to go over just what you need to do to make sure you can successfully seal the deal.

Consider Using A Closing Agent

Some investors might scoff at the notion of seeking such outside help, but tax sales are complicated and the aid that a closing agent can render in tying up loose ends should be appreciated, not scorned. Because even while you are placing your final bid and acquiring your tax lien certificate or deed, you could have your closing agent out there running searches on the title, just in case any last-minute problems should arise. The closing agent will also write up appropriate closing statements and—if necessary—get title insurance for the property.

One of the nice things about closing agents is that they work on a need to know basis, you tell them as much as they need to know in order to get the job done and they typically do not pry any further. Just be sure to get one that can work at a rapid enough pace not to slow the process down. As a rule, your closing agent should not take more than a few days' time to start work on your case. Any longer than this, however, is simply too long to wait.

Make Use Of A Quiet Title

In a perfect world, all titles and transfers of the property would run along smoothly and no one would have any trouble at all. Unfortunately, we all know that this is not the case. And some properties are indeed much more troubled than others. In order to take care of these troublesome properties you just might want to look into obtaining something called a "quiet title."

It's called that because it's a means of "quieting down" any previous complications. If the property is being litigated by local ordinances or the neighborhood HOA for example, you can petition to have this quiet title put into effect in order to momentarily put a hold on any grievances, buying yourself time to sort it all out. Such things could prove crucial as you get ready to close the deal.

Hire Your Own Maintenance

As much as we might like to do everything on our own, the smart investor knows that there are times in which they simply need help. And when it comes to buying property—even under the best of circumstances—there will undoubtedly be a lot of maintenance and upkeep involved. So, don't go it alone if you don't have to. Just put a simple add out in your local paper and you are bound to get inquiries from those interested in handling the maintenance of your property.

From someone to mow the grass to more complex issues such as roofing, plumbing, and electric work; there is plenty of professional, skilled labor to be had. Obtaining property is just the first step after all, in order to really close the deal, you need to have a skilled crew in place to make sure your property is properly maintained for the long haul. Because sometimes a little teamwork can really do some wonders.

Don't Get Sued!

As has already been mentioned in this book, you need to be wary of whether or not a property may have additional liens and judgments taken out against it besides the original lien that may have brought it to auction. This means that even as you are closing the deal and getting ready to take over someone else's foreclosed upon property, you should check up on whether or not there are any further hidden instances of litigation in the works.

Because if you don't you could be on the hook for a lawsuit just waiting to happen. So even as your closing up shop on the auction block, be sure to check up on the history and status of the property so you don't become the proud new owner of a lawsuit waiting to happen. Not a good way to start! So, like always, be proactive, do your due diligence—and don't get sued!

Take Environmental Stock Of Your Property

In order to be a good steward of any newly acquired property, it would be wise to take stock of the general condition of the unit. As mentioned previously in this book, if something appeared to be fundamentally wrong with the immediate location, such as being in a flood plain, or simply surrounded by unconscionable urban blight, it would have been best to have avoided the property altogether.

But beyond these major eyesores, once you become the owner of a property there may be much less obvious defects that might need to be taken care of in order to ensure the long-term health of your investment. If you plan on renting the property later on, for example, you might want to hire someone to check the place for any wayward asbestos that could make tenants seriously sick later on.

And while you are at it, it certainly wouldn't hurt to check for any dangerous mold, lead, or even the presence of radon. Just because you closed the deal, doesn't mean you should wash your hands of the basic environmental state of your property. Such property owners who abstain from carrying out such basic measures, only do so at their own peril.

Learn To Trust Your Gut

Whether you are investing in tax lien certificates, tax deeds, or making a killing renting out property on Airbnb—real estate is a field that requires some fairly rapid, on the spot learning. Sure, you can do your homework and prep yourself for basic contingencies, but quite honestly there are always going to be things that can pop up and catch you completely unaware.

Even right when you are about to close a deal and you think that all your chips are in place, there are always factors that can emerge which catch you completely unaware. It is for this reason that any would-be investor needs to develop a real do it yourself attitude that allows them to be inventive, creative, and able to make on the spot decisions. It may sound a bit prosaic to say so, but it's true—when picking and choosing a property, you've got to just feel it in your gut sometimes.

It's for this reason that many investors find time to be active in other areas of their life that helps them to utilize their capacity to take a little risk. I've got a friend in fact, who mountain bikes because he likes how the sharp turns of the bike paths force him to make quick decisions! At first glance, it might seem a little silly, but whether biking or closing a deal in real estate; sometimes you've just got to trust your gut!

Chapter 4 Potential Risks

No one wants to think about the risks that are associated with their new career or hobby. However, it is essential — especially for Airbnb investing.

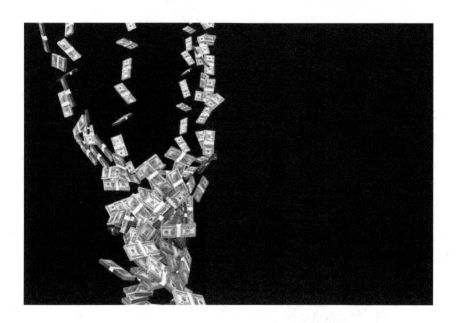

Safety

When it comes to your Airbnb, guests, yourself, neighbors, and any employees, you want their safety to be your top priority. This can be stressful for many people, especially in the beginning. There is a lot to think about when it comes to the safety of everyone. But, the more you realize safety is number one, the easier it is to come up with rules, guidelines and procedures, and handle any situation calmly and rationally.

Managing Strangers

You need to realize that you will manage people you don't know. While most people you will meet are friendly and respectful, there are always people who will not care about your Airbnb. They will not show respect to you or your rental. You want to make sure you have rules and guidelines in place that you and your staff follow. You also want emergency numbers close by, or a way to notify the police, such as an alarm, if something bad happens.

Make sure you have any house rules in place before you start accepting guests. Allow them to view your rules before they agree to stay at your Airbnb. This will ensure that your guests understand the rules and agree to all of your terms. For example, inform them of whether smoking is allowed, how the laundry facilities work, and kitchen rules, if you allow the burning of candles, etc.

You also need to think about your guests' intentions. Are they on vacation for a week, the summer, or just one night? Are they digital nomads who work online and looking for a place to stay for a few days? Whether you are renting a room in your home, or you have a small house you rent and stay close by, you need to think about the reasons for why they are interested in your Airbnb. Unfortunately, with the growth of Airbnbs, a lot of people have started using them to their advantage. Hosts have dealt with robbery and other bad and scary situations. Get to know the people who want to stay at your Airbnb as much as possible before any forms are signed.

This safety factor is not meant to cause anxiety nor scare you from establishing an Airbnb. For the majority of the time, hosts have great experiences with their guests and they hope to meet again. Some guests maintain contact with their hosts after they leave. Investing in any rental property brings up the risks of the safety. As long as you work through the Airbnb website, set your house rules, and make sure that safety is your number one priority, you will have great guests.

Communicate on the Main Airbnb Site

You should always communicate with people through the trusted Airbnb messaging system. Through this system, you are protected from cancellations, refunds, and other problems that could arise. While you have to follow the Airbnb terms of service and payment terms of service, these guidelines are here to help you and your guests. You want everyone to have a positive experience at your Airbnb, and this is one way to ensure that that happens as much as possible.

This site allows you to see your guests' profiles and receive profile verification. You can request that your guests use this, as it allows you to make sure they are who they say they are. You can receive information about your guests, such as their government-issued IDs, email addresses, Facebook profiles, and phone numbers.

The steps are fairly easy to follow to add verification to your account. This is also something that all hosts will want to do for their Airbnb. To verify your account, you need to follow these three steps (What are profile verifications and how do I get them?, n.d.):

1. Go to Airbnb.com and hit "profile."
2. Select "trust and verification."
3. Select a verification to add under the section "add more verification."

Competition Is Fierce

With a quickly growing market, competition is fierce in the Airbnb world. There are nearly 3 million listings for Airbnbs in over 65,000 cities (Khoury, 2018). This brings a lot of competition, especially for people who live in larger areas with a lot of tourism. The best way to get your Airbnb noticed is to make it stand out. You want to do something that is slightly different from all other Airbnbs in your area. For example, you can lower your price a bit, or offer features that most Airbnbs do not. You can even offer a special discount to guests who leave reviews, whether this is 15% off their next stay, or that they will receive a gift card.

You will also want to spend a little more money than planned fixing up your rental. Don't buy the cheapest bedding. Go all out when it comes to the comfort of your guests. Make sure that your Airbnb is clean, and everything you offer is stocked and available. Another tip is to provide brochures to businesses in your community. Some businesses may even make a deal with you that, if someone stays in your Airbnb, they receive a special discount. Get as creative, as you need to make sure you stand out from your competition, but don't allow yourself to struggle financially.

Bad Tenants

Once you start your research on investing in an Airbnb, you will read a lot of horror stories about bad tenants. This is a risk with every rental property and something that needs preparation. For example, you will want to make sure you have insurance and complete background checks of your tenants, especially if you are staying in Airbnb at the same time as them.

While you are covered under the Airbnb Host Protection Concierge, once you sign up, this does not cover every single incident that can happen. Tenants may stay longer than they signed up for, causing problems for your next tenants. They may also damage property or steal from you. Sometimes, you will not notice everything they do right away. Your next tenant might tell you about it, or, one day, you may be walking around your Airbnb and notice an object missing. You don't know when it disappeared. This might seem a bit strange, but your mind gets used to objects sitting around. If you are not paying attention to the object, your mind will naturally assume it is there until you become more mindful and wonder what happened to it, or how long it's been gone.

Some bad tenants are disrespectful and dishonest. For example, a couple of rents from you for two months. You do your best to give them a pleasant experience, but they never seem to be truly happy with your service. Once they leave, they take the time to write a negative review of your Airbnb. They state that you didn't keep the place clean, you became rude, and they felt unwelcomed.

Unfortunately, you can't defend yourself with negative reviews. Instead, you need to note what is said and analyze their stay. If you did everything you could for them, move on from the review. Focus on your past tenants who left positive reviews and future tenants. Even though the negative review is in the open for everyone to read, one negative review generally doesn't keep people away. Most people who are searching for their next Airbnb realize that some people are naturally rude. They look at several, perhaps all, of your reviews, and decide if your place is their best choice.

You can try to do everything in your power to prevent bad tenants, but there is never a guarantee that it will work. You never know who a person truly is until they have signed all the forms and are staying at your Airbnb. This is why you always want to remember to be on guard and protect yourself and your business as much as possible. However, you don't want to fall into the mindset that someone can be bad or dangerous. Take the necessary precautions, but expect people to be kind and respectful.

Legal Problems

If there are people who dislike Airbnbs, it is people who own and run hotels. Since the Airbnb made headlines in 2008, people have started to stay in Airbnbs instead of hotels. This means, especially in some areas, hotels are losing their guests at a rapid rate. Many hotels know that their numbers are declining, and they blame the Airbnbs.

Many hotels brought this issue up in a legal way, and did whatever they could to restrict access to Airbnbs in certain areas. These restrictions are a risk to Airbnbs. When you are setting up your location, you want to work closely with the city, county, and state. You want to make sure that you are following all the rules, guidelines, and restrictions for your area. If you don't, you will face charges or receive a fine. The city can even ask you to close your Airbnb until you follow all the requirements. That can quickly affect your Airbnb, and you will lose guests for some time. Essentially, this means that your rental property is not making money, but you are still left to pay the bills and fines.

Risk Of Vacancy

One of the first factors you should think of before opening an Airbnb is that you may not have tenants constantly. Even if you live in a high tourism area, you can still find your Airbnb vacant for a month or two. You may even have tenants who cancel on you at the last minute, which means you lose the money you were counting on, or you have to issue them a refund.

Most people follow the 24-hour rule. If the tenant alerts you that they need to cancel 24 hours before their check-in time, they are free of any fees. However, if they do not cancel and do not show up, then you will continue to charge their card. When this happens, expect them or their credit card company to contact you, as they will try to get out of the charges. You will need proof that they did not notify you of their cancellation, and need to ensure your policy is in place and that they already know about it.

There are several ways to protect yourself from the risk of vacancy, especially when it comes to quieter tourist seasons. Firstly, you want to thoroughly research the location of your Airbnb. Secondly, you want to think about lowering prices, or doing something special that will make guests choose your Airbnb over another one in the area, especially during low-tourist seasons. Thirdly, you want to always make sure that you have enough cash flow to get you through the tougher months. There are a number of Airbnb profitability calculators to help you understand occupancy rates, capital rates, and cash returns for your location.

Chapter 5 Location Research

When you are performing your research, you may want to look at all the factors you can think of. You will start your research by looking at the best locations, and then find yourself looking at establishing house rules, insurance, and hidden expenses. If you do not organize your research from the start, you will become overwhelmed. This can lead you to think negatively about owning an Airbnb. You might start to feel that you will not succeed because the process is too long, or that you can't afford it.

The first step you want to take when you start to feel overwhelmed is to take a step back. Leave your research for a period of time. It won't go anywhere, and you can return to your computer as soon as you start feeling better. The next step to follow is to take your research into smaller steps. You don't need to learn everything all at once. When people have an idea to invest in property, they want to jump on the bandwagon and start making money as fast as possible. One of the most common mistakes for investing beginners is thinking that they will make money quickly. In reality, it is a slow journey, but once you open your Airbnb, you will quickly notice the benefit, see your bank account grow, and realize that going slowly is much better than jumping into investing.

If you have never spent much time researching, this can feel like an overwhelming task. Fortunately, the research phase is easier than it looks. However, it does take a lot of time, and you may need to spend some money on copies of information and other research fees.

The general research process is basic. You will be following these steps as a guide when you start focusing on your research:

1. Identify your topic.
2. Look for background information in your area and on Airbnbs in general.
3. Start a basic online search for a general idea of your location and tourist information. Look to see what other Airbnbs are in your area.
4. Go to the library, city, county, and state offices to look for statistics.
5. Evaluate all of your research.

Take time to think about your specific research steps. In the space provided, write information on each step to give you a start on your research process.

1. _____
   _
2. _____
   _
3. _____
   _
4. _____
   _
5. _____
   _

Market Research

One of the biggest types of research you will focus on when looking for your location is market research. This looks specifically at statistics and other factors to help you determine the best location for your Airbnb. Because this is a specific type of research, you will need to go beyond Google or Yahoo! for your research. However, these search engines are a great place to start. You will want to go to your city offices to see if there are any statistics on Airbnbs and also gather tourism information. This can lead you to narrow down the best locations for your Airbnb.

Part of market research is looking at other prices of Airbnbs and rental properties people can temporarily stay at. You will want to get an average price and be in the range of this, but you don't want the most expensive Airbnb, especially when you are first starting out. Furthermore, you can't set your price too low such that you struggle to pay bills and save money for repairs.

With market research, you want to understand the difference between primary and secondary research. Primary research is the information that is gotten firsthand. For example, statistics from surveys and reports. Secondary information is information written about previously. For example, if someone writes an article about tourism in your area based on the survey reports, the article is secondary research. The main research you want to pay attention to is the firsthand information. While secondary research can help you, primary research is mainly facts that you can use to choose your best location.

AirDNA

One of the main tools you will use to help you focus on market research is AirDNA. AirDNA will give you the information that you will not find anywhere else. The data collected and placed into AirDNA comes from the Airbnb website. AirDNA can feel overwhelming at first, but it is essential that you look into this database. This is a tool that you want to use often, as it will help you grow as a host. You will understand more about the Airbnb world, what your guests want, how to manage your investments, guests, staff, and make the right decisions. AirDNA helps you understand that your business will grow, but this will take time.

Identify Your Competition

Through your research, you will need to identify your competition. You will do this through your primary and secondary market research. You can find Airbnbs in your area by doing online research, the Airbnb website, and the statistics and reports of your local governmental offices.

It is important to realize the rate of growth when it comes to the Airbnb community. There are hundreds of new locations added to the Airbnb website daily. You want to keep up with your competition. You don't want to focus on your competition during your beginning research phase. You want to pay attention to all the new Airbnbs in your area, what the current prices are, and what services they offer. People are constantly changing their Airbnb, and it is important that you keep up with your competition.

Understanding Listings

Another part of your market research is making sure you understand the listings. You can learn a lot about running your Airbnb by looking at the current listings in your area and surrounding areas. For example, if you are opening an Airbnb in Florida, you will want to start by looking at a 25-mile radius from your possible location. You will then expand to 50 miles and even look into neighboring states.

There are four main parts of a listing (What factors determine how my listing appears in the search results?, n.d.):

- Price. The prices of other Airbnbs in your area will become the deciding factor of your Airbnb price. You might not want yours to be the lowest price, but you will want to be cheaper than most, especially in the beginning. You will need to create a budget to ensure that you can make the bills and still have capital every month, but you do not want to be the most expensive Airbnb.

- New listing. The Airbnb website lists the newest listing first when they show up in searches. The website is available to help you establish your business. They will use algorithms to ensure your listing is noticed when people are searching for accommodation in your area.

- Reviews. Reviews are incredibly important on the Airbnb website and for your business. The more reviews you have, the more people will notice your Airbnb. You should highly consider not only asking people to leave reviews, but also giving them a coupon for a local business or a discount for their next stay for leaving a positive review.

- Superhost. Once you pass certain requirements, the Airbnb website lists you as a superhost. This is a high honor, and one that people look for when they are searching for a place to stay on their vacation.

These listing factors are important for you to notice in your research and remember throughout your process. Take a moment to highlight or write this information down. Have it available when you need a reminder, especially when you are starting to create your advertisements and listing your Airbnb on the website.

Best And Worst U.S. Cities For Airbnb

The housing market in your area can make or break the chance of establishing an Airbnb. For instance, there are many states where purchasing a home is too expensive. This causes people to rent instead of buy. Of course, you can always make a deal with your landlord to get them on the same page with your Airbnb idea.

However, if you are serious about becoming an Airbnb host and willing to go anywhere in the world to make this happen, then you will want to choose one of the best locations for Airbnb rentals (Saldana, 2019).

Best Places for One- and Two-Bedroom Properties

- Nashville, Tennessee. Monthly rent is $1,380 and arbitrage potential is $1,663.

- Des Moines, Iowa. Monthly rent is $810 and arbitrage potential is $1,190. (One bedroom properties only.)

- Honolulu, Hawaii. Monthly rent is $1,700 and arbitrage potential is $1,746.

- Boston, Massachusetts. Monthly rent is $2,400 and arbitrage potential is $1,520.

- Detroit, Michigan. Monthly rent is $610 and arbitrage potential is $1,273.

- Corpus Christi, Texas. Monthly rent is $1,070 and arbitrage potential is $1,620. (Two bedroom properties only.)

Worst Places for One Bedroom Properties

- San Francisco, California. Monthly rent is $3,700 and arbitrage potential is -$455.

- New York, New York. Monthly rent is $2,850 and arbitrage potential is -$302.

- Laredo, Texas. Monthly rent is $830 and arbitrage potential is -$285.

- Oakland, California. Monthly rent is $2,270 and arbitrage potential is -$295.

- San Jose, California. Monthly rent is $2,850 and arbitrage potential is -$412.

Worst Place for Two Bedroom Properties.

- Irving, Texas. Monthly rent is $1,490 and arbitrage potential is -$399.

- Chandler, Arizona. Monthly rent is $1,440 and arbitrage potential is -$263.

- Scottsdale, Arizona. Monthly rent is $2,080 and arbitrage potential is -$403.

- Oakland, California. Monthly rent is $2,720 and arbitrage potential is -$89.

- Laredo, Texas. Monthly rent is $940 and arbitrage potential is -$230.

Chapter 6 Analyzing A Rental Property

Enthused about profiting by Rental property anyway scanning for an alternative rather than agreements, dispossessions, inhabitants, or flipping Rental property? Gaining the benefit to assemble on criminal Rental property charges can be an advantageous theory even with confined capital.

Areas all things considered assess charges on Rental property to owners consistently and consider portion by a particular date. The bills are assessed reliant on property estimation and can keep running from two or three hundred dollars to a couple of thousand dollars. If they are not paid when due they become criminal and the area can charge interest. In various states, the areas are allowed to dole out their privilege to assemble the bad behavior to an examiner.

Exactly when the property owner pays the toll to the area, the examiner gets their basic endeavor notwithstanding the interest. The reasonable interest varies by zone anyway continues running between 5-18 percent for every annum all around. If a property owner fails to pay the bad behavior inside the necessary time allocation the examiner can begin methods to gain a deed to the property. Evaluation liens generally take need over all other property commitments, including contracts.

Before causing the endeavor through and through to explore the property to certify it is appealing and to sidestep any issue properties. Be certain the estimation of the property far outperforms the locale obligation bill. A general standard rule is a property estimation at any rate on different occasions the aggregate owed.

It is basic to comprehend the strategy and systems will move fundamentally by zone and that not all states look into cost lien bargains. Moreover, recollect there is a difference between evaluation lien verifications and obligation deeds. Control and obligation regarding property are only possible through an obligation deed after any predefined recuperation period has ended.

For example, in Orange County, Florida obligations become criminal for non-portion April 1 of the following year. The area by then conveys the leeway of announcements in the paper during the extended length of May.

A charmed examiner can enlist to offer on the supports at the deal. Rather than an "up close and personal" auction, the offering as of now occurs on the web. Bidders must store 10% of the aggregate they plan to proceed with the area. Orange County can charge 18% on delinquent evaluations so the offering starts at this most noteworthy and is offered down. So a bidder ready to secure 10% would persuade a bidder needing 12%.

A triumphant bidder pays the zone for the proportion of delinquent obligations and obtains their appearance when the bill is paid by the property owner (the territory keeps the qualification in eagerness between the total accumulated and the money related pros winning offer). Budgetary pros owning supports that have not been paid or recovered by the owner for a period of two years can apply for an obligation deed bargain. The greater part of property owners deals with their delinquent tab before it goes to the deed compose. This empowers theorists to secure strong returns upheld using Rental property. Right when an owner fails to pay, it is serviceable for a budgetary pro to guarantee a property worth a large number of dollars for a theory of just two or three hundred dollars with much greater benefits available for resale.

This present downturn of 2008 to 2010 has really destroyed the protections trade which has compelled various individual budgetary masters to reevaluate their hypothesis needs. A significant part of these monetary authorities is starting to look for elective kinds of contributing, one of which is Rental property.

By and by I know there's been a hotel showcase crisis that has mirrored the money related trade crisis from various perspectives, anyway, the truth proceeds as before that at present may be a perfect chance to get by and by into Rental property contributing. Expenses have dropped altogether, once in a while as much as 30 or 40% on properties regardless of what you look like at it in practically every region in America. That is my technique for uncovering to you that there are some amazing courses of action to be had right now which just pledges to give indications of progress as time goes on.

Today I have to examine two or three ways to deal with profit by the present Rental property contributing condition and give you a couple of things to focus on that you probably won't have thought of by and by.

Today likely the best detect that we're seeing to place assets into Rental property incorporates different family structures with up to 10 units. It's optimal to place assets into these different family structures just in towns that you starting at now live in. Do whatever it takes not to endeavor to buy a couple of these scattered the country over in light of the way that with our present economy they may take more thought and greater affirmation on your part to get them up and productive which means owning one in the town you right currently live is going to make things considerably progressively basic for you, in any occasion until further notice.

The mind-boggling favorable circumstances of these sorts of hypotheses are that they're minimal enough to be supervised by the owner, you. One thing you're obviously going to need to examine before you purchase is available laws concerning these sorts of structures.

Various towns have rent control laws similarly as non-removing laws that make it fundamentally progressively difficult for you to discard tenants that aren't covering the tabs. Without a doubt, this may be the explanation the present owner has had so a lot of issues that they have to sell. You can't make an advantage if your inhabitants don't pay their rent and you can't expel them without consuming a considerable number of dollars in authentic costs and various extensive stretches of time.

However, in case you can find one of these speculation properties in your general region and there aren't any unpleasant laws that would impact you, by and by may just be the perfect time to swoop in and get it. Do whatever it takes not to be humble about offering ridiculously low expenses in light of the way that various money related experts are planning to sell at any expense to get out from under their home credits.

Numerous speculators obtained the properties with variable or movable rate home loans back when things were great and are presently finding that they can't renegotiate those advances on the grounds that the present condition of the economy and the present condition of the financial market which is viably frigid credit for some individuals.

So there you have one straightforward approach to benefit in Rental property, notwithstanding during a downturn.

With the current money related atmosphere the manner in which it is, speculations are searching down for financial specialists around the world. Financial exchanges are not working out quite as well and thusly nor are the assets which contribute there. Gold has turned out to be too costly to even think about purchasing as are numerous different assets. That doesn't leave speculators numerous spots to get a decent return. With the exception of one kind of venture, the well established ensured approach to get an arrival - Rental property.

Customarily Rental property has been probably the most secure speculation, particularly long haul. There is constantly a requirement for lodging, and regardless of current money related markets, your venture is constantly protected and will quite often increment. Obviously, when we talk about Rental property speculations, numerous individuals will think about the family home, however, there is more cash to be made in this industry.

The most well-known manner by which individuals profit in Rental property is by buying the home or condo and renting it out to others for a charge every month. Presently this might be too long haul inhabitants which are considered, more secure as the month to month rental expense is increasingly steady. Or on the other hand, for lofts or homes in prevalent visitor goals, there is a rental charge for each night or week. This sort of occasion settlement will prompt a lot of higher expenses, yet this may not be as steady, particularly on account of occasion goals with down occasions, (for example, winter in certain areas).

The two regular strategies where individuals pay for Rental property speculations are as per the following. For those with a lot of fluid money, they may possess the property through and through. This recoveries from paying any intrigue and will mean any rental payment is coming directly into your pocket. Anyway, for other people, who don't have them out and out capital or wish to possess many occasion homes, different banks and individual credits can be utilized to buy the property. With these advances, one may pay the 'contract' during each time with the rental pay (as this will diminish the intrigue you pay). Others utilize the idea of intrigue just credit, which is the place they just pay the enthusiasm of the advance and never any of the head. In this circumstance, the arrival on venture comes when the time has come to sell the Rental property. You should be cautious about this kind of credit and be certain the property cost will build every year with a higher rate than the intrigue you pay.

Regardless of how you choose to pay for Rental property speculations, be guaranteed they are an extraordinary cash creator and sure to bring upon an arrival. On the off chance that you take a gander at a portion of the independent moguls around the globe, you will see something normal between almost every one of them. They profited inland ventures and property improvement. Frequently beginning with one property these insightful financial specialists make such exceptional yields that they are before long controlling numerous properties and even their own high rise structures. Start your adventure today and put resources into the land to make a benefit.

Numerous individuals are thinking about venture realty to have something they could get cash from. It is tied in with making benefits that you also can get yourself into. Step into the Rental property business world and produce proceeding with income with realty venture.

No degree or any instructive accomplishment is required to have realty for speculation. All you need is cash that will fill in as your capital and the correct information, which you can acquire even without taking care of a school. Appropriate learning on realty speculation can be gotten any place you are, even at home as long as you most likely are aware where to get supportive data or courses on the web.

As a potential realty financial specialist, it is basic for you to figure out how you can diminish all costs included and boost your income. You need to survey all that might be engaged with your endeavors like the rental rate, rental payment, property fix costs (current and future use), the profit that you can get in the event that you sell your property and quantifiable profit.

Starting in speculation realty isn't simple. Discovering venture realities can be so exceptionally testing however with the correct skill, appropriate instruction, key arranging and compelling techniques, you can clearly deal with and manage nearly everything without problems. On the off chance that you are longing to produce proceeding with a stream of money with the realty, try to stay up with the latest with the most recent patterns in realty venture and what can be normal later on.

Likewise, you need to discover yourself exactly how you can build up your net an incentive with a speculation realty that you can control. Other than purchasing a limited reality, there are numerous different things that you should consider other than low market worth cost. Numerous realty financial specialists are thinking about dispossessed homes that they can embellish and sell at a market worth cost.

In spite of the fact that dispossessed realties can be an achievable venture methodology, despite everything you must be cautious in deciding their good and bad times as now and again, these properties can just cost you more. A large number of these properties require costly fixes and exorbitant remodels. Being a financial specialist, you need to perform assessments either without anyone else or with an expert at that point get gauges for whatever expenses might be associated with improving the property.

You likewise need to make sense of when you can anticipate an arrival on speculation. On the off chance that your picked realty will just the motivation you to continue going through for a year as opposed to picking up inside three or four months, discover another venture realty and consider different methodologies that can give you incredible benefits.

You need an operator who has a decent notoriety and who acts rapidly for your benefit. For instance, will they demonstrate your property rapidly if a purchaser needs to see it? The operator who sold me the property I currently live in, wouldn't demonstrate it to me for 48 hours as he was too busy.... When I advised the seller - she happened to cut the garden at the front of the property, and I halted to talk with her - she was angry with him. She was paying him all that commission and he wouldn't set aside the effort to demonstrate a purchaser round in an auspicious way. I don't know whether that specialist is still in business, however there are some brilliant models that I can discuss having encountered them with the operator who sold me that house.

Most importantly, he was a liar. He advised the merchants that they needed to go out while he held an Open Home for imminent purchasers. I happened to drop by after the Open Home and I saw that no one had gone to his Open Home, yet he told the dealers that individuals came to the Open Home.

With this specific arrangement, I conflicted with my very own recommendation of never being the principal individual to name a cost. I was so amped up for the property, that I offered a significant expense at the start. After the arrangement was finished the operator revealed to me that no one else would have offered such a significant expense for the property. I felt horrendous. Be that as it may, in a resulting exchange with the merchant, he made me feel somewhat better by saying from my point of view, I think you got a lot. From your point of view, you think you paid a lot for the property. Be that as it may, it was a great learning background. Try not to be the first to name a cost, do your exploration, yet even as the purchaser or the dealer, attempt to arrange a superior cost.

As the dealer, know that in the event that you have given the specialist time limits for him to be the sole operator before it goes on a numerous posting, they are regularly edgy to make a deal with the goal that they don't need to part their bonus. So regardless of whether they have done due industriousness, they are still prone to guide you to bring down your cost by 10% or 20% to get individuals keen on coming, and after that attempt to constrain you into selling route underneath the value you needed to acknowledge. Presently, when it goes on a various posting, in a decent economy your specialist probably won't put in a ton of exertion attempting to discover you a purchaser. In the downturn economy, they might be frantic enough to take the necessary steps to get you a purchaser, including utilizing harassing strategies to get you to bring down your asking cost. They don't stop for a second to utilize the dread factor. On the off chance that you don't sell it at this value, you might clutch it for an extensive stretch of time. In the event that you do offer it at a much lower value, we'll have a greater amount of a chance to sell it for you.

A customer of mine was convinced to sell her home at closeout. She truly didn't know whether she needed to go that course, however the operator persuaded her that she could presumably go anyplace from $525K to $585K for her home - that it would be a speedy deal, she would get her cash, it would be finished. Spent over $5K on publicizing which the operator had coercively proposed, and after that the day preceding the property was to go to sell, the specialist called her and advised she expected to set her to save cost at $450K and that she would be fortunate in the event that she even got that.

This is such a gross absence of trustworthiness. They pull off this constantly. At no time when he was forcing her to put her property up at sale did he reveal to her that she would likely need to endure a shot of $130K. She accepted it with little or no evidence that she would leave the arrangement with a benefit. Rather, on the off chance that he had his direction, he would have gotten the commission and she would have continued the misfortune. She came to me directly after the operator called her advising her to decrease her asking cost. She was in tears since she had just made an idea on another property believing that she would have the cash from the closeout of this house. I prompted her not to proceed with the bartering. So when she went in there that equivalent night and disclosed to them she wasn't proceeding - they stated, God helps us, you can't do that. Also, she stated, gracious yes I can, you're not getting my mark thus you can't sell my home.

Remember that specialists make their living from bonuses on deals. The commission depends on a level of the deal cost and is determined on a recipe the operator ought to unveil in many nations, in the event that you inquire. Like everything else in Rental property, it is debatable! Talk about the commission before making or accepting an offer.

The best time to deal over commission is the point at which the gatherings are near the point that it is just the commission that is standing out. Remember, operators are especially eager in the downturn market, and multiple times out of ten it fills in as they would very much want to sell a property and make some commission than let the deal fall through and make nothing by any means.

To summarize:

- guarantee that your operator will demonstrate your property in an auspicious way if a forthcoming purchaser turns up
- attempt to get suggestions for an operator who has uprightness and who is straightforward
- don't be rushed and don't get scared. It's your property, you're the one in control. Eventually, somebody will purchase your home.

Chapter 7 Getting Funds Needed for Wholesaling

After going through the negotiations process to seal the deal on the seller's property, you need to cover the property under a contract so that you can then further refer it to someone on your VIP Cash Buyer's list.

Contract Assignment Method

Assigning is considered as the mainstream method of wholesale funding. Assigning is passing on the right to purchase a property to another person for a small fee that is considered as an assignment fee. You will be removing yourself from the deal that you have worked for and signing over the rights of the property to the cash buyer that will be providing the backend funds to attain the property. The cash buyer is already aware of all the terms and conditions and the terms within the purchase and sale agreement that were finalized with the motivated seller. Hence, the backend cash buyer is now responsible for the property. They then come forward and complete the final processes leading up to the transaction, so the deal is finally closed while you wait on the sidelines to be paid as the deal is finally sealed, and afterward, you get paid.

You need to have some information to write down within the purchase and sales agreement which will be the name of the seller, the address of the property that is being sold, the telephone number of the buyer and the telephone number of the person who is selling the property and a mailing address of the seller that can be checked out in order to send mail regarding taxes. These keywords need to be the focus of your purchase and sales agreement that you need to have jotted down to assign the rights of the property that you want to buy to the backend cash buyer. And or assignee statements let the seller know that a potential back end buyer might step into the scene to purchase the property.

A Step in a Backward Direction

You need to remember some values that you will have to negotiate to make a substantial profit from the wholesale process when you are trying to complete the purchase and sales agreement with the motivated seller.

You will have to negotiate the purchase price and how much the earnest deposit will be. Also, negotiate where the closing should commence. Should it take place with Escrow or your friendly real estate agent? If you go with Escrow, then finalize the date of the Escrow. Also, consider mentioning who the closing cost is going to be paid by and also talk about when a period of inspection will take place.

If your negotiation skills are excellent, you will have made a significant profit and savings, and you will lean toward the following statements. You will have purchased the property for the lowest possible amount. The buyer will have paid the closing costs. The earnest deposit will have been the least amount that could be refundable during the inspection period in case some discrepancies arise, which normally would not occur. You will have got an inspection period that would satisfy you. And the closing of the deal will have happened with your investor-friendly real estate agent. To make this seem easier for you to understand, we could take an example to analyze the situation better. You presented the low offer of about one hundred and five thousand dollars to the seller because you felt as if the ARV would amount to more than two hundred and fifteen thousand dollars while including costs for a forty thousand dollars rehab of the property due to damages to the property. You also paid all of the closing costs within the time limit of twenty days, and you also presented a fully refundable earnest deposit of around a hundred dollars to make sure that the contract is fully secure. The closing agent that you have selected from the So and So named company would be responsible for handling all the paperwork, and you persuade the seller to arrange an analysis of the property over a ten business day period so that you and your team can easily inspect all the fine details regarding the property the seller is selling. You and the seller reach a final agreement and make sure to spend around fifteen minutes to fill in all the paperwork regarding the purchase and sales agreement. You may now proceed to take decent pictures and videos of the real estate, and in case the property is also vacant, you could persuade the seller to install a contractor's lockbox to the property in case you and your rehabber team needs to come in early to start with the inspection of the subject property and start to make plans for the rehabbing of the property. If the property has residents inside it, you should make sure to notify the seller whenever you need to make inspections of the property so that the seller and his family can give you access to the whole house without any problems and without causing any inconvenience for them. Inform them that you might need to come back several times within the inspection period that lasts for about ten business days. By the time you have entered into the contract with the seller to buy the property, you should start presenting that deal around on different forms of advertisements to get the word out and to attract back end cash buyers for the property. You need to make sure to do this as fast as possible because as the contract has been signed, your ten-day period of inspection has already started. The ten-day inspection period can be a decent way to escape and back out of the deal in case any problems arise, and you can get your earnest deposit of a hundred dollars back as well.

For example, the assignment fee for the contract has been put up by you like ten thousand dollars, so you will have to market the property at around one hundred and fifteen thousand dollars. You will now have to put some bandit signs around the property that state that the house is below fifty appraisals and that you only accept cash buyers to purchase the property, and then your number and the title heading should be something that advertises the property as a special deal.

You should now design a flyer with your automated advertisement system that you have bought and make sure to post it on the page of your Facebook account. Then move over to another site like Craigslist and put up an ad for the property as we discussed earlier in the book. Then, you should drive toward your local investor-friendly real estate agent and present him with the purchase and sales agreement for the property and proceed by opening up Escrow and do not forget to present your earnest deposit due to one hundred dollars as well. Be sure to make the most out of your trip to your local investor-friendly real estate agent in case of any heads up regarding cash buyers who are eagerly waiting for some good deals on some good properties to hit two birds with one stone in a sense.

Considering you have already got some VIP Cash buyers on your list, do not forget to inform them of the property that you are selling for the discounted price.

Make sure to email text, voicemail, and broadcast to them regarding the deal that you are presenting to them as a limited time offer with your marketing system.

Now that you have informed all of your VIP Cash buyers about the property that you are selling, it is time that you wait for the offers to come in slowly. Make sure to answer all of their questions and persuade them that the house that you are selling is their dream house. Make sure to indicate that the property might sell quickly to reel them in faster. Present to them pictures and videos of the property that you had taken prior. If they are interested in purchasing the property so far, make the most of this opportunity and make sure you present to them the offer to inspect the property in person and schedule a time with them for the inspection. Be sure to analyze all the tire kickers and anyone who does not seem to have any money to purchase the property in the first place to avoid any difficulties in wanting to sell the property. Also, persuade them to do a drive-by to make sure they are interested in buying the property or not before you spend time hanging out with them for the inspection of the property. This will filter out time-wasters that could pose as a waste of your valuable time.

Some basic terms and conditions that you want to go over during every deal when selling to the cash buyer under an assignment are the assignment fee, which is around ten thousand dollars in this case. The earnest deposit is around a thousand to three thousand and five dollars in this case. Make sure to arrange a closing date before your original closing date. Make sure you also use your closing agent to seal the deal with you selling the property to the cash buyer because the escrow has already been opened.

After searching for a cash buyer who is ardent about purchasing the property, you just need to fill in a one-pager about assigning the contract to him and for him to take the deal instead of you. Assignment of Contract is a typical one-page contract, and it only requires a few minutes to fill in, which declares that you have passed all the rights of the property to the buyer who has acquired it from you. The cash buyer now has to go over all the original details of the original purchase and sales agreement and know about all the details regarding the property. After going through all the details, the cash buyer now has to confirm the deal and agree to the terms and conditions. The cash buyer now has to just go through the process of filling out the form for the assignment and provide the non-refundable cash deposit over to your closing agent and then turn it in. After this happens, you can sit back and finally relax as you are finally out of the picture and have successfully cleared your role as a wholesaler. You need just patiently to wait for your ten thousand dollar assignment fee.

The Benefits of an Assignment

Assigning the property to a cash buyer helps you save money. You originally agreed to pay the closing costs with the seller, but now that the cash buyer is going to replace you in that role as the seller, those ordeals are transferred over to the cash buyer, meaning you do not have to pay for the closing costs anymore. You're free to assign the property for a set amount, and you can easily calculate the profit as a wholesaler

Assigning the property is easy and fast. It just involves you and the cash buyer signing a single-sided piece of paper that is wrapped up in a few minutes.

It is easy to assign and sell the property to a cash buyer. You found a great deal at around half the market value of similar properties, and you served it on a platter for ten thousand dollars so you could easily sell it to a rehabber who is serious about acquiring the property. What they care about is if the property that you are selling to them is according to what they want out of a property and that they can make a significant profit out of it.

The Downside of Signing off Property

You are completely transparent when it comes to making a profit. Everyone that is involved within the deal whether it be the seller of the back end cash buyer, everyone will be aware of the profit that you have made and if you made a hefty profit, both the seller and the buyer might end up irritated and disappointed that you made a large amount of profit without doing any work while they had to do most of the work. This could potentially ruin the deal that you were trying to make. You need to make sure that you are making around ten thousand dollars and also make sure to maintain good relations with your cash buyers.

Make sure not to strain the relationships that you have already formed as these do come in handy in the long run in most situations. As you progress on your wholesale venture, your relations with your cash buyers will be stronger, and they will proceed and continue to appreciate the decisions you take and allow you to take the lead because you continue to bring profitable and good properties to them. As time progresses, the deals that you can make will be easier, and assignments of properties to back end cash buyers will become easier and easier all the time that your cash buyers learn how to do business with you

Double Closing

Now that you have learned how to process the assignment of properties between yourself and your potential cash buyer, you need to also learn about a slightly difficult and complicated method of selling properties, which are known as the Back-to-Back close. In this method, you, yourself, are using the cash buyer's back end money to fund the purchase from the seller with the overages becoming your profit as a wholesaler. This could be explained with the transition principle as A-B and B-C, so it could be considered as A-C where A could be considered as the motivated seller, and B is the wholesaler of the property, and C is the cash buyer wanting to get a good deal out of the investment.

We will now have to consider another example to explain how the double closing process works. You negotiate to purchase the property from the seller for a hundred and five thousand dollars because the ARV would have caused the price to be around two hundred and fifteen thousand dollars after considering an approximated rehab of about forty thousand dollars. You, as you previously did, agree on committing to a hundred dollar deposit to make the contract secure and to the title company to pay the closing costs. As before, you have an inspection period of around 10 days, and you will have to close the deal within 30 days

Instead of wanting to make just a mere ten thousand, say you want to make around an extra ten thousand meaning your total profit will be around twenty thousand dollars, so you would have to market the property at around a hundred and twenty-five thousand dollars by using the techniques that have already been listed down in this book. You contract the property for around a hundred and five thousand dollars with the seller. So the purchase price would amount to a solid hundred and five thousand dollars. You would make an earnest deposit of a hundred dollars, which would be refundable only within the ten-day inspection period, and it would be non-refundable afterward. You would choose the closing location to be your investor-friendly agent's office with a close escrow of around 30 days.

This could be considered the A to B side of things where you are purchasing the property from the seller, and as soon as you acquire the contract you opened an escrow with your closing agent, so now you have an equal amount of interest in regards to the property, but you should start marketing to sell the property to a cash buyer for around a hundred and twenty-five thousand dollars now.

Now, let us hypothesize that you have found a cash buyer willing to spend a hundred and twenty-five thousand dollars on the property that you want to sell. You will send them a purchase and sales agreement, which constitutes a purchase price of a hundred and twenty-five thousand dollars. You would specify the closing location to be your investor-friendly closing agent's office again, and the earnest deposit, which would be non-refundable, would be around two thousand and five hundred dollars. The close of the escrow would be around twenty days or less, and the cash buyer would have to pay the closing costs

So the paperwork that you create is a bit lean in your favor, and you make sure to send it over to the cash buyer to get it signed by him. After getting him to agree with the terms, you visit your investor-friendly real estate agent to get the closing done and open up the escrow by handing over the Purchase and Sales Agreement that has been signed as well as the non-refundable earnest deposit. You now have the cash buyer sealed within the deal, and this can be considered as the B to C part of the transaction.

If you have kept track of what you have been doing, you have now opened up two escrows, one escrow where you were supposedly buying the property of the seller and one where you are selling the property to the back end cash buyer. Think of it as cash flowing like water from one part of a stream to another part of the stream. Once the cash buyer decides to close, they will now deposit their one hundred and twenty-five thousand dollars into the escrow, and your closing agent will make sure to allow only one hundred and five thousand dollars to be transferred from the escrow into the escrow where you were buying the property from the seller, and that will fund your purchase.

As the A to B escrow is closed out, it is your closing agent's job to now clear out the B to C escrow and hands over the twenty thousand dollars that you were supposed to get while deducting the closing costs. In the end, it is a win-win for everyone as the cash buyer is happy to get a discounted property at around a hundred and twenty-five thousand dollars, which is up to him to keep or to rehab or sell for a profit. The seller is happy to have got a good deal out of his property for around a hundred and five thousand dollars. You are also pleased with the wholesale as you have now made a respectable twenty thousand dollars of profit from the property by not needing to use any of your money.

The Advantages of Double Closing On A Deal

You are invisible to both the buyer and the seller because you separated both the buyer and seller from the buying and selling process, and now you can gain a hefty profit from the deal without both the buyer and seller ever finding out about it.

The Downside of Double Closing on A Deal

The problem now is the payment of two closings as there are now two separate closing costs for the property. You can get your back end cash buyer to pay for the B to C set of closing costs but traditionally the wholesaler makes the payment of the A to B set of closing costs which can range from anywhere between a thousand dollars and five thousand dollars which directly depends on the transfer fees of the state where you are carrying out the closings.

If you think about it, the whole situation is quite complicated. Before the crash of the real estate market from 2006 to 2007, closing simultaneously was a trend, and closing agents were aware of this trend and would allow for this to happen, but the crash led to many closing agents leaving the closing business as a whole. New policies and regulations controlled how closing agents would have to do business after the whole real estate crash crisis. Theoretically, double closes are still the norm and still legal, but due to the unfamiliarity of the whole double closing procedure and some of them downright not allowing them, most closing agents do not consider partaking in double closings. So, wholesalers that are new to the wholesale and real estate scene might be misinformed by closing agents that double closes are considered illegal, and that could pose a small but significant hurdle for them. If you come across a closing agent who informs you that double closing is against the state policy and has been considered illegal for as long as a decade, do not take the time out to argue with him but instead thank him and try to find another closing agent and form decent ties with him; one who is aware of how double closes are done and allows them. Inevitably, you will find an investor-friendly real estate agent that allows them

Everything Is Coming Together

You are now aware of how to locate properties. You have now made a VIP Cash Buyer's list, and you are now able to calculate values and costs and are able to carry out negotiations like a professional, but now you need to figure out how to efficiently fund deals using other people's money also known as OPM.

Chapter 8 Finding Property That Is Prime for Flipping

Once you familiarize yourself with the generalized process of house flipping, the players involved in it, and the documents you will be frequently signing, it is time to start looking for a property. Locating property prime for investing requires a combination of instinct and science. First, you will need to find an in.

Finding an "In"

Having connections in the world of real estate is not only an advantage, but it is also critical to your success. It is important to build yourself a network of other investors and real estate professionals. First, introduce yourself as a buyer in the market and find an agent. Tell the agent that you intend to flip the house. A good agent will be able to put you in touch with others who may benefit from the connection. After some time, you will become familiar with other investors in the area as well. Although these people will sometimes be your competition, it is important to view them as potential helpers as well. Sometimes you will encounter a property or opportunity that is not right for your investment style, but maybe perfect for a fellow investor with whom you are familiar. That same investor may eventually find himself in a similar situation with you in mind sometime in the future. View your competition as friendly, not hostile.

Auctions are another great way to find potential flipping property while familiarizing yourself with the local investment players and their hierarchy. After attending a few auctions, you will know who the power players are and have an idea of what it will take to survive in your local investment scene. You will also know what it will take to secure properties to flip in your area and how far your dollar will go. Do not become so involved in your observations, though, that you forget to mingle. Striking up a casual conversation in a setting as informal as an auction is a great way to begin forming your network. It can also be a good approach to get to know some of the lawyers and accountants in your area who specialize in real estate.

Good old-fashioned newspaper classifieds can also be a great way to get your foot in the door. Look for classified ads that use taglines such as "We Buy Ugly Houses" or "Cash Now for Your Homes." Chances are, these are investors like you who are fishing for houses. Call the numbers and ask questions. Introduce yourself. You may initially be greeted with a bit of repressed hostility, but you just might make a friend who can provide you with some invaluable insight. When you feel the time is right, go fishing yourself by running a few ads of your own. You will get some curious inquiries, but you also just may convince that one homeowner who is desperate to unload a potential gem to sell to you at the right price.

Join a professional organization and attend a convention. Conventions and seminars are a great way to begin networking. Not only can you meet others in the business, but also you often get the opportunity to hear some of the most successful members of the community speak on what helped them succeed as well as what did not. The National Association of Real Estate Investors (NAREI), for instance, is an organization that offers the assistance of mentors, as well as educational opportunities and workshops to its members. Making friends within an organization of like-minded professionals is not only beneficial, but it can be profitable. Advertise. Let people know that you are looking for properties in which to invest, in order to lead potential sellers to you. Put up an advertisement in the classified section of your local periodical stating that you are an investor looking to buy a property. Have business cards printed up and capitalize on every opportunity to pass them out or display them. Begin taking contact information from local For Sale signs in the area and directly contacting the selling agent. Discuss with him or her about your goals. Most agents are motivated by potential clients and good ones are great informational resources.

Sponsor a local youth athletic team in a community recreation league and advertise in tournament books. This sounds rather trite, but it actually has far-reaching subliminal impact and is usually a somewhat inexpensive marketing ploy, typically less than $200. People may not necessarily realize that they are registering your business name every time they see it screen-printed across the jerseys of the team you sponsor, but when the time comes for them to utilize your services, they will often recall the name of the business that sponsored "the team with the purple shirts." In a way, this type of advertising works very much in the same way as paraphernalia for political campaigning, but research has proven that when voters know nothing about the candidates vying for a specific political office, they will cast their vote based on name recognition. Simply put, people choose what they know. Similarly, community members may not know that much about real estate, but if they spend twelve weekends in the spring and fall looking at your name splashed across the shirts of local youth and in the pages of tournament books as they try to figure out whether Junior's team is going to make it to the semifinals, they will know your name when the need arises. This greatly increases the chance of their calling you versus a random business name they pull out of the yellow pages. Finding your first property is typically the most difficult. However, once you find yourself away in and establish your team of professionals and contractors, your success is completely in your hands. You are limited only by the restrictions you place upon yourself.

Identifying Neighborhoods of Opportunity

Although when you first begin to consider a career in real estate flipping, a specific neighborhood may immediately pop into your mind, choosing an area in which to focus is not always as obvious as it seems. Chances are, many of the hot neighborhoods in your area that are currently experiencing a renaissance of some sort are probably already overflowing with investors. In such cases, it may pay off more in the long run for you to do some research in order to determine what area may become the next new "it" neighborhood, and focus your efforts there. Investment properties are probably going to be costly in an area that is popular, and even retail buyers, who would otherwise prefer a home that is in move-in condition, may be willing to compete for a fixer upper for the opportunity to live in a neighborhood that they might not otherwise be able to afford.

In choosing a neighborhood to focus your flipping efforts, every beginning investor is faced with the problem of whether to buy the best house in the worst neighborhood or the worst house in the best neighborhood. Either could be the correct answer, depending on the situation. It is true that the more undesirable the neighborhood is, the smaller your potential buyer's market will be. Quite simply, fewer people are willing to take risks for even the best house in a neighborhood notorious for crime, poor schools, or mostly rundown homes. However, if that neighborhood happens to be going through somewhat of a renaissance, people may be more willing to take the chance in exchange for the opportunity to get in on the ground floor of a boom that promises to explore the value of the property within a few years. Therefore, the best bet for locating a neighborhood ideal for flipping homes is to locate an older neighborhood in town that is on the verge of rebirth. You can determine this, not merely by following home sales and property notices in the area, but just by following the development trends. If you begin to notice a fair amount of new retail or commercial businesses appearing in the area, that may be a good sign that the economy of that neighborhood is on the rise. Pay attention to local news features or stories that announce plans for new shopping centers, restaurants, or entertainment complexes.

If you do not already have a subscription to the local newspaper, get one. Checking the classified section should become a daily routine. In addition to checking the advertisements of homes for sale, you should also read the public notices. Public notices will include bankruptcy, foreclosure, and auction notices. Take a drive. Drive around potential neighborhoods and pay attention to the general upkeep of homes in the area. Pay attention to the cars parked in the driveways or on the streets. Are they newer or older? If you are driving around during a business day, does there seem to be an unusual number of cars parked at their homes? Evaluate the neighborhood for its proximity to places of convenience such as gas stations or grocery stores. Search for other selling points for the area such as mature trees, wooded lots, etc. Make a mental note of the type of people you see out and about. Does the neighborhood appear to consist primarily of younger families, empty nesters, or young professionals? This will be your market demographics when it's time for you to sell. As you peruse prospective neighborhoods, make a mental note if there seems to be an unusually high number of For Sale signs in the neighborhood. This could be a red flag for some sort of underlying issue in the neighborhood and may warrant further investigation.

Once you narrow your neighborhood search down to a couple of prospective locales, start regularly checking the MLS ads for those areas. The Multiple Listing Service is a database of all properties for sale in a geographic region that is specifically targeted to real estate professionals. The MLS contains such information as square footage, a breakdown of room sizes, property tax information, annual homeowner's fees (if applicable), school district, and the condition of the property. The MLS database will help you create a comparative foundation for what houses are selling for in the area and how condition is affecting selling costs. It can also help you establish a base for how long houses are generally staying on the market before being sold, which is important when each month your property goes unsold is costing you another mortgage payment. One aspect of MLS worth mentioning, however, is that in some cities, the MLS database is freely accessible to anyone with an internet connection while in other cities some of the information is restricted to real estate professionals. If you live in a city that does the latter, you will need to have your agent provide you with regular information from the MLS.

It is worth addressing the fact that, although some investors do not restrict their business to a single neighborhood or even city, it is not recommended that you begin your career on a national or international level. Conducting multiple and continuous real estate transactions across state lines requires a certain level of skill, experience, and expertise that requires a seasoned professional with a great staff and an even better attorney, because you are no longer dealing exclusively with the laws of one state, but many. Expanding to an international scale is something that should be considered very carefully. Although you will see many advertisements promising cheap real estate in foreign countries, it is important to remember that it's just as important to be familiar with the area in which you wish to buy in an another country as it is on your own. This implies that, before you even start to consider purchasing a property in a foreign land, you will probably need to take multiple scouting trips, which, depending on the country in which you are considering investing, can become rather expensive very quickly. Once you determine that you would like to own property in that country, you will also need to familiarize yourself with the real estate laws of that country. This often involves a lot of bureaucratic red tape that is best and most efficiently dealt with by hiring an attorney licensed to practice in that country. Finally, once you own a home or piece of land in a foreign country, before you even begin any type of work on it, you will need to understand the local regulations for renovations in that region as well as the customs and processes for employing workers. In short, it can become a rather complicated bureaucratic process that is best handled by third party professionals whom you hire, which will require quite a bit of pocket change. The good news is that, just as in your own country, once you find your "in," you are in. However, the cautionary advice being offered here is to ensure that you have plenty of time and funds before you even begin to think nationally or globally. In short, it is usually best to start at home and expand outward.

Scouting

When you are out driving neighborhoods, do not only look for houses with For Sale signs in front of them. Look for properties that show signs of being vacant or are unusually unkempt for the area. Look for overgrown grass and landscaping that has not been maintained, notices taped to doors, or boarded windows. Sometimes these properties are prime targets for flipping opportunities. These homes could be involved in estate escrow as the result of a death, going through the foreclosure process, occupied by the very elderly with no relatives nearby, or owned by someone who has encountered financial difficulties and may be motivated to sell. If you locate a property that interests you, watch it regularly. If its status does not change or it continues to decline, begin checking city or county records to check the status of the home. Interview neighbors to see if they can give you any further information. This process is called scouting.

How does scouting work? It can actually be as simple or as complicated as the individual acting as a scout chooses to make it. In its simplest form, a scout can simply be the errand person for an investor—someone he or she sends out to search for available properties in a specific neighborhood. This type of scouting may simply involve searching for homes that may be on the open market, but not necessarily advertised in the most lucrative manner, such as homes for which the owners are acting as the agents. Another type of scout acts on his or her own terms and then proactively seeks investors who may benefit from the information gathered. These individuals will locate properties that are in disrepair and appear to be unoccupied and are not currently listed on the market, and they will visit city and county records offices to locate the owners. They may then contact those owners directly to see if they might be motivated sellers. If they are, the scout then has a potentially viable flip for an investor that is not available to the mass market, since the owner is not actively seeking to sell the property.

One word of caution to would-be professional scouts, however, is to remember that a good deal of your integrity will rest on your ability to deliver. Therefore, it is important that you can deliver what you promise. In order to do this, you must be very good at reading people. If an owner agrees that he or she may be interested in selling simply from the pressure to do so, that owner may not turn out to be such an avid negotiator. Although the investor to whom you shopped the deal may become frustrated with the owner, he will be equally frustrated with you, because you brought this deal to the table. If you plan to earn a decent income as a scout, then it is important for you to form partnerships with investors, which you do by carrying through on your promised product. Expect to earn more of a part-time income as a scout when you are first starting out. Since scouts merely sell information and have virtually no involvement in the real estate transactions themselves, they naturally earn the least amount of any of the parties involved. A few hundred dollars for a good lead is typically considered a fair price. One benefit of being a scout, however, is that you are technically a service provider and not a real estate professional, and that means you escape many of the pitfalls of the tricky real estate laws when tax season rolls around.

Chapter 9 Real Estate Investment Deals

When it comes to investment properties, the most commonly asked question is where a person can get funding for the next deal.

If you are thinking of purchasing a house for investment, but you don't have sufficient money in your bank account, don't worry. Fortunately, there are many financing opportunities than you know. Picking the right choice for your investment strategy and specific instance save you a huge amount of money.

In this section, you will learn about the various loans available for financing your next real estate investment.

1. Conventional loans

This is one of the most common types of mortgage. In a conventional loan, you pay a certain amount of money before the bank provides you with the remaining money. Although a lot of banks let borrowers pay as little as 5% of the buying price, investors have no option but to put down more than that. As such, many investors pay a down payment of 20%, so that the loan is not considered as part of the private mortgage insurance. (PMI).

Advantages

- Easy to understand
- The most common type of financing, so it is easy to shop around for the best terms and rates.
- Conventional loans are one of the lowest interest rates for any loan options.

Disadvantages

- Conventional loans have a limit.
- You require to have a credit score of more than 640 to qualify.

- It is a bit difficult to qualify if you purchase properties using LLC instead of putting them in your name.

2. Veteran Affairs (VA) loan

Getting a VA loan is a great achievement of working in the military. This loan provides no-down-payment loans to veterans, chosen military spouses, and service members. Same to FHA loan, you will have to stay in the home for a minimum of one year. One good thing with this type of loan is that you can purchase as many houses as you would like as long as you don't surpass the set amount, and you stay in each one for a minimum of one year. The limiting aspect isn't the number of houses; it is the amount you are awarded.

Advantages

- PMI not needed for VA loans.
- It has the lowest interest rate.
- No down payment. Very low closing costs. With the VA loans, the seller will have to pay for some of the closings costs the buyer would always pay.
- A high ratio of debt-to-income allowed.

- You can correctly develop a portfolio of rental properties without any down payment by living in every house for a year, or renting out each and moving on.

Disadvantages

- Not available to everyone.
- You will need to live in the property for at least one year.
- A lot of paperwork at the time of settlement.
- There is a specific VA funding charge that is included in your loan that the VA asks to ensure the program continues to run.

3. 203(k) loan

The 203(k) loan resembles the FHA loan because it is centered a lot toward homeowners than investors. This is an owner-occupied, 3.5% down payment loan that lets you lump the rehab costs into the mortgage.

Advantages

- You can support the entire project with one lender.
- You can expand the choices to include distressed and foreclosed homes.

- You can request a better deal on a property that deserves rehab, which means you can gain immediate equity.

- If you do the rehab work yourself, you can move on to discuss the costs below the retail process.

- No need to look for additional money for rehab costs, and when you are done, the home will possibly be worth more than the loan amount.

Disadvantages

- Contractors have to be voted and approved by your lender.

- Only accessible to owner-occupants- you must live at the property as your main residence.

- In general, the amount of paperwork is more during and after settlement.

4. Private money

This one refers to finances from individual investors. There are no institutions involved here. In this method, you can ask for support from family, co-workers, or a few close friends you have interacted with at your local real estate investing groups. In general, private money will be costlier than a traditional mortgage. However, the terms set are more flexible. Additionally, the requirements to qualify for this type of funding is friendly.

Pros

- Minimum qualifications are demanded.
- Has a simple and flexible structure.

Cons

- Has a higher interest rate than other loans.
- You may need to look for an attorney to create a financial contract.
- The terms are shorter (3-5) years.
- In case things don't go well, it may destroy the relationship between you and the lender.

5. Hard money

This resembles private money; the only difference is that the money doesn't come from an individual but a hard-money lender. For this type of loan, the lender uses a hard asset to protect the loan. Hard money is a form of short-term loan used by borrowers to purchase fix up and flip. In general, you can get hard money to account for 70-80% of the property bought before rehab. Just like private money, hard-money lenders cut a huge interest and include other charges such as origination fees.

Pros

- It is easy to get because the loan is protected by property.
- Has a simple and flexible loan structure.
- Lenders of hard money know the special needs of real estate investors and provide quick loan funding and approval.

Cons

- The rate of interest is higher than other loans.
- It can be quite expensive if a person is thought to be risky.

There are many methods to employ to finance your real estate investment deals. Understanding everything about each method is crucial. It is important that you consider all the available options rather than jump into traditional methods of financing. Find time to discuss your methods and choices with a professional loan officer who has interacted with investors and develop the best financing plan for your situations, knowing that those situations change over time.

The world has people who are looking for great places to invest their money. Therefore, if you have a good record of generating profit with your real estate investment, then getting a financing option will not be a big problem for you. You may need to become a bit creative.

Find the best deals and the investing strategies

People continue to join real estate to generate wealth, and the more people want to purchase real estate properties, the harder it becomes to find deals. It is that simple as supply and demand in business.

As a result, the method that investors employed to find deals in the past is quickly changing. Unlike a few years ago where it was possible to get a deal using MLS, today is almost impossible. But instead, smart investors are redefining their methods of finding deals. At the end of the day, if you want something that no one else can get, it is a must that you do something that no one else will do to earn.

So, are you ready to learn what to do what everyone is not doing? If yes, here are a few methods that you can apply to strike a great deal.

Let's start!

1. Try to purchase foreclosed properties from a bank.

When a person fails to pay his or her mortgage for a certain period, the lender will decide to repossess the property and chase away the occupants. Once the house is empty, the lender goes on to list the house for sale on the market, by using a local real estate channel.

While foreclosure is a sad thing, these homes can be one of the best deals you can come across in real estate. Banks will always want to remain in the business of lending money, and not maintaining homes or houses, so they are always quick to provide massive discounts just to remove the deal from their records. But though these are one of the best deals ever, you can only strike a great deal on foreclosed properties, if you know the methods of purchasing foreclosures.

Since the foreclosure process requires different years; these properties require serious updating and repair. In this case, more discounts may be generated to compensate for the buyers.

2. Make sure you are the first or the last.

In the real estate business, the early bird always catches the worm. Sometimes, it is not the highest offer for a property that is accepted; it's but the first. As a result, if you are searching for a great deal, you must be quick to snatch it. Look for pre-approval from a bank so that you can jump at any property anytime, and let your real estate agent set you up to receive automatic email alerts reminding you of new property that comes to the market.

Next, don't wait for anything but check it out immediately, and send an offer the same day if you can.

Alternatively, you can also find the best deals by looking at properties that have been in the market for a long time. The owners of these properties are usually ready to sell for a discount because they are tired of holding on to the same property. In most cases, they may have been making two mortgage payments and will accept any offer.

3. Look for absent property owners privately.

In a competitive real estate, great deals can be very difficult to find because of the huge number of people hunting for a house. In some places, a single home for sale may receive more than a dozen offers in the first few days.

As a result, the best trick real estate investors employ today to get in touch with contact owners and ask them to sell. At any moment, a great percentage of the population will listen to this option, so why should you not reach out to them before they list it with a real estate agent?

The best people to focus on are absentee owners; these are individuals who own a given property but don't live there. They could be landlords or owners who have inherited their houses and are not sure what to do with them. You can get these deals in different ways, such as:

- Purchasing public record list.
- Searching for houses that appear vacant.
- Making a call to mom-and-pop landlords who have listed properties "for rent" on the Craigslist. Tell them that you are not interested in renting the property, but you would like to speak with them about purchasing.

4. Eviction records

Evictions aren't a good thing. It is messy, time-intensive, and costly. During the time of eviction, many landlords start to ask questions about why they are involved in this game.

This is the reason why focusing on landlords who are in the process of an eviction can be so good. They are experiencing a problem, and there is a good chance they will be happy to get out of the property quickly.

Well, how can you target these landlords?

Evictions are an aspect of public records in many counties of America. This means that you can visit your local county administration office and request to see a list of the current evictions happening. Various counties and states conduct evictions in different ways, but if you ask it shouldn't be difficult to find.

5. Direct mail

Lastly, you must recognize that finding the best deals is possibly a 'numbers game.' So if you have a list of people who can be your potential sellers, you can decide to send them letters, having the belief that a small percentage may call you to discuss, and a few of those may end up selling you their properties.

Although this may look cheap on the surface, direct email marketers know that the proof lies in the percentages. Lastly, if you remain passionate about your goal to find sellers, then you will possibly find many. One thing that you must know is that people are always ready to help you accomplish your goals, you need to let the world know what you want, and the rest will help you get it.

How to analyze deals and make offers?

As a real estate investor, you can either build or destroy your investment when you pay a lot for a property; you may end up losing all your shorts. Find a great deal on a home, and it may make a big difference.

Some programs exist that promise you to get deals from the comfort of your home. As long as you have a stable internet connection, a computer, and a telephone you are in business. But remember when the deal is so good, think twice. The truth is that there is a lot that is done apart from playing around with numbers.

While feelings can dictate whether you will buy a property or not, there is a lot more than just your feelings. Typically, you want a real estate deal that will fulfill your goals. To realize that, you must know how to analyze and value the property, including predicting whether it's going to generate money.

Your responsibility as you assess various properties is to ignore the list of prices, or what the sellers might want and concentrate on what is important to you.

Don't be scared about the property assessment of the city or whether the sellers paid for it. Those numbers aren't that important. You might use them while negotiating if it comes to that point, but for the sake of analyzing the property, they are not necessary.

As you assess the property, pay attention to the following things:

- What is the place zoned out for? What else can you add there? Can you create an office space or more units?
- Are there any regulations or rules set on the use of the property?
- What are the forms of transport near the property?

- What status is the property in?
- Are there any problems caused by the environment near the property? This can be bed bugs, earthquakes, termites, mold and many more.
- Who are the occupants? Owners of the property or tenants?
- What else is in the area that is attractive for someone living there? Does it have parks?
- What is your gut telling you when you set eyes on the property? How is the experience when you are on the property?

Some of the things mentioned here you can check using google maps and gather other information from the internet. However, many of these questions require that you show up physically in the property to answer them accurately.

Next, to determine the values, you will require to run the same analysis on other properties that are on the market, including the ones that have been sold recently in the area. You will also need to look for time to calculate the rent rate you can earn for the property.

In case you find two properties with the same size and location, but one is more expensive than the other, it is your task to find out why. Remember, the cheaper property could be in a worse location. Or it could be in a noisy street, or close to a garbage dump where it receives less sunlight. These are just a few of the many things that you will have to figure out.

Things you need to analyze a real estate deal and compute the cash flow

You will require to collect most of the following information to determine the cash flow:

- Property taxes.
- Property maintenance
- Recycling/garbage fee
- Rent
- Electricity
- Heat

Aside from this, you will need to develop a rough idea of how much you will require to pay as a down payment. Most of the items listed above can be estimated until you receive an accepted offer on the property, at which point you will have an easy route to the real numbers. But the more actual numbers you get from the seller and your different sources, the more accurate your cash flow prediction will be.

Ways to determine whether a property is a great real estate deal

Every property buyer wants a great deal while buying a real estate. Although the price is important, finding a property that can be destroyed with the least effort and time cannot be that easy. Anyone who buys a house with the purpose to fix it up to understands that there could be hidden challenges that arise without warning and aren't easy to identify, even if you have the best home assessment. The ability to tell whether a house is worth its investment requires a keen eye. Here are tips that you can use to tell whether a property can be a great deal.

1. Determine zoning problems and liens

In general, one way that you can know is when a property has a complication that may result in automatic "no" for most investors. Zoning problems and liens on a little non-institutional grade property are the best spots.

2. Stick to the 1% rule

There are different methods to review an investment return when purchasing an income property. As a rule of thumb, clients are advised to use the 1% rule that demands the income property should rent for around 1% of the buying price to generate positive cash flow.

3. Review the CAP Rate

Cap rate is one great signal, although there are some sensible reasons for a few sellers to become motivated than others. Also, the price per square foot or the price per door vs. neighborhood comps as good metrics if used well.

4. Look at the roofline

This can help you to see if the house appears sturdy, simple, elegant, vulnerable, or weak.

5. Develop a sense of condition and presentation

The status of the property plus how it has been presented will determine whether the property can be bought at a discount. So, in case, the property doesn't have an online photo, then it probably has a zero-curb appeal. It also implies that a substantial discount can be asked on the buying price and the listing agent doesn't have a lot of work to do, and may just after a quick sale.

Chapter 10 Buying Your Property

Real estate represents a significant portion of many people's wealth, and this is especially true for American homeowners. More than 50% of American families are said to own personal property. The popularity of this industry does not seem to be waning anytime soon, and it is an attractive and lucrative sector where many investors show interest.

Different factors determine the value of a property in the real estate market. One of the more costly mistakes that people make in home buying is the neglect of research and proper preparation. You need to start looking out to understand the kind of deals that are best for you.

The internet has made it easy to go ahead and get full of the details about your desired home from the comfort of your device screen. This means that sellers can showcase the value of a house and provide informative and helpful information. The goal of every buyer is to purchase a fantastic home that will satisfy all of their needs.

Understanding the real value of a house isn't as easy as it seems. You need to ensure that you consult with your team to ensure that the value of the property is as high as it can be. This consultation does not mean that you should overprice the property; it merely means that the right price (based on the value of the property) is gotten.

House flipping professionals understand the importance of including certain features in the property. To prosper in this industry, you need to know how competitive the market is. This understanding will help you to maximize your money and use it for essential inclusions.

Factors that Affect the Value

Location: The location of a property is one of the most important factors that buyers consider. This is why you need to ensure that you carefully study the area and determine where properties are being sold at a quick pace. The ideal location can be the differentiating factor between success and failure when it comes to house flipping. If you are a retailer that is seeking to flip property, then you should be looking at neighborhoods that have thrived for a couple of decades. This kind of community will have well-maintained homes as it is home to mainly middle-class earners. When you are also looking for the ideal location, you need to look away from the declining area of town. Apart from the attractions, homeowners want to have an assurance of safety and the lowest possible crime rates. All these factors into the ideal location, and to have a fair bargain, you need to consider them.

Demography

This refers to a set of data that is used to describe the composition of the population in a particular area. Data such as race, age, gender, population growth, income patterns, and the population growth of a specific area are crucial. Although these statistics are often overlooked in other areas, they are critical ways to access the value of property in real estate.

Demographic factors also affect the kinds of property that are in demand. These factors also affect too often over the existing real estate trends and potentially influence the real estate market.

When it comes to the property itself, certain upgrades can be made to improve its value.

General condition

The general condition of a property is a crucial factor that goes a long way in determining the value of the property. If a property is in excellent condition, then you will minimize the amount of capital that you require for flipping. The general situation is also crucial because it determines how much time will be spent making these improvements.

You should go for homes that are in good condition if you want to make a significant profit on your flips. However, over the years, I have come across individual houses that are like gold, found in the rubbles. It takes experience and foresight to see them

Although you can get an excellent bargain for properties that are in poor conditions, it is hardly ever the better route. When it comes to houses, the price of repairs may eventually outweigh the presumed profit. There are certain areas in the home that need to be checked appropriately during the process of buying in.

Let's run through three of these things:

The Roof: The cost of roof repairs varies based on certain conditions relating to longevity and the quality of materials used. In some cases, you may have to apply chemicals to solve minor problems like discoloration.

Plumbing: The proper functioning of the plumbing system has to be checked. To assert the level of repairs that you have to make, you need to know how long the materials have been in use

Wiring: This is one fault that is not always as obvious unless you pay attention to it during the process of inspection.

Apart from external factors, individual factors affect the value of the house. This is why, over time, flippers have focused on upgrading certain parts of the home to improve the value.

Cellar Conversion: The conversion of an already existing cellar to living can boost the value by as much as 30%. To maximize this flip, you need to ensure that the build cost per square foot is less than the price per square foot of the area. Cellar conversions are some of the less complicated home improvements that you can make. It is also a great option because this improvement makes it qualify as a "change of use." Therefore, you may not need planning permission (however, you may need to talk to your local planning officer).

Splitting: This involves the conversion of a house into separate units. It is a real estate technique that is popular in London. To ensure that you get it right with splitting, you need to do your research to check if there's a demand for flats in that area. For example, if you notice that three-bedroom properties aren't moving as fast, you could consider conversion.

Garage Conversion: This could be a great option if the property has adequate parking space. You can add value to your property by turning an unused garage into a living area. The creativity that is involved in this process largely determines the cost that this flip will add to your property. By doing this well, you can improve the value of your property by up to 15%. In most cases, a garage conversion is seen as permitted development, and therefore, it doesn't require planning permission. To do this rightly, you need to check that the garage is suitable for conversion and subsequently get planning permission if you need to.

Increase living space: You can also increase the living space in a property with a conservatory. To make the best of this sort of flip, you need to ensure that you pick the right kind of glass and glazing options. In terms of regulation, this kind of flip is seen as permitted development, and to get it right, you have to learn the conditions and limits. It is also good to seek advice from experienced agents and other experts.

Kitchen: The kitchen is another part of the house that can be extended to improve value. You can gain valuable space by continuing the kitchen into the side return. This is also a great way to improve the layout and give the kitchen that modern and comfortable feel. However, side extensions will cause you to lose the light that windows bring in (roof lights or a glazed roof are worthy alternatives). To get it right, you will need to ensure that you comply with building regulations. There will also be inspections at crucial stages of the project to ensure that the finished extension is in line with regulations. There is no doubt that kitchen repairs will give you some of the most significant returns on investment.

An extra bedroom: This inclusion alone can increase the value of your home by about 15%. How can you get a spare bedroom? One classical answer to this is by converting the loft. There are hardly any lofts that you cannot convert, and you need to employ the services of the right architect to double-check and be sure about it.

New bathrooms: Having a modern bathroom will undoubtedly increase the value of a property. A lot of people assume that it is an expensive investment, but then, it is an investment that will surely yield returns. For many people, a bathroom update is highly impactful on the value of the property. The value increase happens because areas like the bathroom and kitchen are both high use areas. When it comes to flipping the bathrooms, you do not always need a complete renovation. You may include some new fixtures that will change the look of the bathroom without breaking the bank.

ENTERING THE MARKET

As we mentioned earlier in the book, it is essential to have objectives in place. These objectives will guide you through your career in real estate, and they can be changed and adjusted from time to time. After you must have determined what your entry strategy is, the next step is to determine the kind of property that you seek to find. Subsequently, this will determine the price range of property that you may consider.

To become a thriving investor in this field, you need to ensure that you have clearly defined objectives. This does not only apply to the short term, but you also need long-term objectives too. You must determine whether you want to be a scout, or you want to be a dealer or a full-time flipper.

You will need to ensure that you do not let your emotions get the better of you when you make decisions about

With the proper plan, you will find it easy to map out your success strategy in advance.

MODE OF PAYMENT

The method of payment is one crucial part of the flipping process. You can use the pattern and urgency of payment to negotiate deals. From the seller's point of view, some benefits come from paying cash. Every buyer wants to be faced with the least obstacles when it comes to doing business. Therefore, buyers who pay with cash can gain the upper hand during negotiations. Why do sellers like all-cash offers?

If you are trying to purchase real estate, you can get it for a lower price if you choose an all-cash purchase. Lenders often require an appraisal before the closing, and if this value is less than the mortgage amount, then it can lead to complications.

When it comes to purchasing property, even buyers who are qualified for home loans can face scrutiny. With cash payments, there is no need for appraisals or any of the other multiple contingencies. A buyer's qualification for a mortgage can change based on changes in the financial situation.

For example, a person who has not been fully employed in the same occupation for two years or someone who was a victim of identity theft may have issues securing loans.

Cash sales are also preferred because they typically take less time to complete. Once the home inspection is complete, then you can close the deal in less than a week. Lenders who have multiple foreclosures in their portfolios discount the list prices. This is done with hopes of attracting more offers. In the end, customers who offer cash for real-estate-owned homed tend to win most offers.

Apart from the negotiating strength that cash payment provides, it also means that you do not have to make mortgage payments every month. It also means that in case of a financial emergency, you can make use of the equity that the home provides. Irrespective of the level fluctuations in the market, owners without a mortgage have access to 100% equity.

Lastly, when you offer cash payments for a property, you take away any restrictions on the title transfer.

LOCATING THE RIGHT PROPERTY FOR YOU

Success in house flipping only comes when you find the right property to flip. This is not always an easy task because it requires patience and due diligence in your search. When you find the right property, you can mitigate risks while maximizing profits (isn't the goal for any business?)

How can I find the right property?

There is no particular rule regarding how you can find the right property for you. It is best to always get a large pool of options by putting your ears on the ground at every point. I would suggest that you work with leads from various real estate agents.

You can also stay in touch with the latest listings through classified advertisements. You can find these in the real estate columns of your favorite newspapers and magazines. In looking out for these adverts, you may check for words that show the buyer's level of seriousness. Phrases like motivated seller connote that such a seller may need to make sales urgently.

Several platforms post both local and regional details about listings. Once you check out these platforms regularly, you are bound to find several potential deals.

Networking and human relations are essential for anyone that deals with real estate. Another way to find the right property for you is by becoming a part of an investment club. Various cities have clubs (and these clubs also have regular publications), and these clubs are made up of professionals. You are likely to find architects, brokers, engineers, real estate attorneys, and many other professionals. Within this group, you are likely to get information that will lead you to your ideal property.

Apart from sharing information, members of these kinds of groups often meet periodically to network and learn about the business. These kinds of events are great for anyone that is starting in the flipping business.

FSBOs are also another great way to find great deals on homes for flips. For sale by owners (FSBO) is a situation where the owner of the house is directly involved in the process. There is a tendency that you can use this to your advantage and get amazing deals from these kinds of people.

Chapter 11 Finding Pre-Foreclosure Properties

Let's discuss foreclosure:

Types of foreclosure

1. Judicial foreclosure: A judicial foreclosure means the foreclosure must be processed through the state's court system.
2. A non-judicial foreclosure is also known as a foreclosure by power of sale. In this method, the sale takes place without the supervision of the court, and the lender can invoke its right to foreclose by filing a notice of default.

Buying properties from people in foreclosure

You need to know two things about property owners who are behind on their payments. First, many owners will look for a way to keep their house before selling it. Secondly, the majority of homeowners will owe more than the property is worth. In these situations, you can negotiate a short sale with the homeowner and the bank. A short sale is when the lender/mortgagee agrees to accept less than it is owed on the existing debt as payment in full.

You will face challenges when buying properties in pre-foreclosure, such as:

1. Lack of professionals: Know what you are doing. Understand the process from start to finish. This knowledge will increase your chances of success.
2. Unskilled negotiators: You need to be an effective negotiator so you can convince lien holders to take discounted settlements.
3. Conflicting interests: Working with the conflicting interests of attorneys, agents, creditors, and the need of the homeowner –

combined with a short timeline – is tough. You need to create a win-win situation for all.

4. Late arrivals: You need to get in front of the homeowner in foreclosure as early in the process as possible. Experienced real estate professionals reveal that this can positively affect your success rate.

5. Emotionally charged: Selling a property in foreclosure is often emotional for the homeowner. Be empathic to the homeowner without getting caught up in the emotions of the situation.

Understanding the pre-foreclosure process is critical when dealing with sellers who are going through this experience.

Finding recent pre-foreclosure property filings

You can get a pre-foreclosure list:

1. You can create the list by going down to your local county government office and finding the recent notice of default filing or lis pendens.

2. A pre-foreclosure list provider can sell it to you.

Going to the local county office in person is ideal. By going there, you can take advantage of the clerks' knowledge and gather other lists. A lis pendens is filed in judicial foreclosure actions. On the other hand, the notice of default is filed in non-judicial foreclosure actions. Here is what you can gather from these documents:

- Date of the lis pendens or NOD
- Names and addresses of the mortgagor in default
- Name and addresses of the mortgagee foreclosing on the loan
- Case or notice default number
- Date of auction or trustee's sale
- Property address
- The outstanding balance at the time of case filing
- Amount in default
- Date last payment was made
- The date the loan was made
- Loan amount

- Property's tax assessment
- Property's zoning detail
- Property's legal description or "Schedule A."

Making friends with the clerk is a good idea because they can be a great source of information. They can help you explain the documents you need. The clerk may even know the best local pre-foreclosure list provider from whom you can search by the list each month.

You can find pre-foreclosure property filings from the following sources:

1. Newspaper: You can find your state's publications from this website: (http://www.mypublicnotices.com/PublicNotice.asp). Additionally, foreclosure notices are published in the locally circulated newspaper.
2. Online: Search " ….. country notice of default or lis pendens records." A visit to your clerk's office can help you find online sources.
3. Pre-foreclosure list brokers: A number of pre-foreclosure list providers, and data broker services sell pre-foreclosure data to investors

and other real estate professionals. Subscribe to one in your area. This website is helpful (https://realeflow.com/)

Marketing to property owners in pre-foreclosure. Here are a few ways you can target pre-foreclosure properties:

- Place Craigslist ads targeting pre-foreclosure properties
- Create targeted pay-per-click campaigns
- Create Facebook ads
- Do outdoor advertising
- Utilize the Multiple Listing Service (MLS)

Direct mail and pre-foreclosure door packets are two proven ways to get a response.

Chapter 12 The Bold Offer

You get either one of these two when making an offer: An acceptance or a rejection. Some property investors see this part as a scary thing; they end up not attempting to make an offer on a piece of property but rather stick to the ones they already have. The reason why these property investors get scared about making an offer is that they have never dealt with certain difficulties that surround making an offer on a rental property. This chapter will teach you how to eliminate fear while making an offer on real estate. You get to learn the things you need while preparing for an offer and how not to get a 'no' from the real estate property seller.

The How

You already know factors to consider while venturing into rental property investment, and you already know your teammates. By now, you also know what you will be settling for; you know the type of property you will be buying and the right location to find it. What you are probably planning to do now is make an offer.

If you do not make an offer in the right way, you will likely get a 'no' for an answer. First, you have to know who will receive your offer before knowing how to make an offer. When it is time you make an offer, it can be through a private seller or through an agent/agent.

Private Sellers

If the property you plan to buy is not listed in the Multiple Listing Service (MLS), then you will be dealing with the private seller. Properties that are not listed in the MLS do not need real estate agents when it comes to making an offer. It is something you can deal with all alone. The offer you make to a private seller is not official at first because it all starts with a verbal offer.

You and the private seller get to negotiate and eventually agree on a particular price. All you need to do to make it official after concluding on a price is to get an official purchase document and a sale document where you both sign all necessary papers. If you want to make it less official, you can get a 'letter of intent.' A letter of intent is a non-legal document that briefly states all the important facts. You and the seller then need to draft an official purchase and sale agreement. You can get an official purchase and sale agreement for free from a local title company, from websites that sell legal forms, or from an office supply store. If you do not want to go through any of these avenues, you can make use of an attorney. Using an attorney may be quite expensive but this may be the best time to make use of the attorney you have on your team.

Agents

If you are buying a house listed in the MLS, you cannot escape going through a real estate agent. Usually, there are two agents you have to go through; one agent represents the seller of the property while the other represents the buyer of the property, which is you. You do not have to pay both agents; the owner of the property pays them. It will be the joy of the real estate agent you have on your team to represent you. Having your own agent work with you can make things easier and faster, as they will guide you on things to do while making an offer. Your agent gets to deliver the signed offer to the other agent himself or herself, and then you both await a reply.

You can also make use of the same agent that represents the seller; that same agent helps encourage the seller of the property to give a positive response to your offer as soon as possible. However, this approach is not for you if you are an inexperienced investor. At times, using the same agent may not be favorable because the same person is working for both the buyer and the seller. Sometimes, the agent tends to work in favor of the seller, especially when he or she has promised to sell the property at a higher price, which may not turn out to be what you budgeted for.

If you think you have enough experience and can get a 'yes' as quick as possible, the idea of making use of the same agent is not bad.

What You Should Know When Making Your Offer

You have to know the following when making an offer:
- What do you plan to purchase, and how much does it cost?
- Who are those involved in the offer?
- How do you plan to finance it?
- When is the closing date for the purchase?

- What will make you terminate an offer?

By now, you know what you want to buy; you know the best property that suits your taste and your money. While making an offer, you should have a pre-knowledge of what the property you are buying costs. You should not be ignorant about what is going on in the real estate market. Is what you are about to buy worth it?

Who are those involved in the offer?

It was explained earlier in this chapter that your offer could be made either through agents or through a private seller. If you are making an offer on a property in the MLS, you should know by now that you will be making your offer through agents.

If you are going for a property that is not in the MLS, then you and the private seller are the parties involved in the offer.

How do you plan to finance it?

Although not all offers submitted requires this, many sellers do. It is likely you see a seller that is interested in knowing how you plan to finance your purchase or the kind of financing you will use for the purchase. They want to know where you will be getting funds. Is it from conventional financing obtained from a local bank? Will you be paying with private money? The reason why sellers ask a series of questions is to know how you plan to pay for the property and how long they will have to wait for you to pay. Most sellers are scared of having an offer being terminated because of issues with funding.

When is the closing date for the purchase?

If you are making your offer, you should state the date and be very conscious of this date. One of the reasons why some property investors fail is because they do not stick to the closing date due to failing to be prepared.

What will make you terminate an offer?

Lack of financing can make you terminate an offer; some problems noticed during inspection can make you terminate any offer or if you learn that the property is not worth what was offered.

After paying the earnest money deposit, you do not terminate an offer just because you feel like it. You will learn how to legally terminate an offer discussed in this chapter.

Your Earnest Money Deposit

The Earnest Money Deposit (EMD) is a term used in a real estate transaction; it is most times paid when a purchase and sale agreement is signed, and the EMD is sometimes attached to the offer made. EMD is not the complete amount of money you used in purchasing a property, but it means a deposit made by you to the seller of the property to show such seller that you are serious about buying the property.

The earnest money is a pledged deposit; therefore, if you do not have a legitimate reason for keeping your own side of the pledge, you lose your money to the seller. The only right way to break your own part of the pledge is if it is stated in the purchase and sale agreement that you can opt-out if you find something that seems to be a problem with the property, have financial constraints keeping you from your own end of the promise, or if you eventually notice that the property's appraisal is far less than what you offered.

How much do you have to deposit?

In most cases, there is no specific amount to deposit, but there are some sellers that require a specific amount from you. Therefore, earnest money depends on the price of the property and the seller of such property. Most times, the earnest money deposit is 1% to 2% of the purchase price itself; it all depends on the market. You can decide to deposit more than that, but be careful not to deposit too huge of an amount of money so as not to be at a loss if something eventually comes up. However, paying more than the required percentage does not only show how serious you are, it also gives you a higher chance of getting a 'yes' from the offer.

If your seller is a motivated seller, they do not care about the amount you should deposit; in fact, they often do not see it as a necessary thing for you to do. Therefore, you can decide to deposit any amount to show your seller how serious you are.

Who should keep your earnest money deposit?

If you want to be on the safer side, it is advisable that you give your earnest money to the attorney in charge of the closing or the title company and not the direct seller. Doing this ensures all terms and conditions that apply to the earnest money are adequately followed.

What happens to your earnest money deposit?

All depending on how you go about the deal, there are three things that could happen to your money: it could be lost, it could be retrieved, and it could become part of the closing money. Each of them is explained below, so as a smart rental property investor, you should know how to go about the deal.

It could be lost: Losing the money you deposited can be a very painful thing, especially when the money is a bit much; therefore, if you will not be buying that property at the end of everything for one reason or the other, it can be costly. So as not to lose your money, you have to have a legal reason for breaking the deal. To legalize your reasons, you should add up anything that may cause you to back out of the purchase and sale agreement. If you do not have a legal reason, then forget about your money. The only way your money can be returned to you is if the seller willingly decides to return your money or if you already have a cordial relationship before the buyer-seller relationship.

It could be retrieved: The only way your money can be retrieved is if you have reasons already stated in the purchase and sale agreement. If the transaction eventually becomes unsuccessful, you have every right to collect your money from the buyer if you wish to.

It could become part of the closing money: If the transaction becomes successful at the end of the day, the title company or attorney that will help with the closing will ask you to balance up during the closing. Therefore, the earnest money will be added to the initial price you agreed to pay for the property. For instance, if the agreed amount of the property is $1000 and you paid $100 for the earnest money deposit, you will be asked to balance up with $900.

Secrets Of Successful Offers

There is nothing as sweet as getting a 'yes' to an offer, but you do not just get a 'yes' easily, especially when you find yourself in the competitive market; there are some secrets you need to know. These secrets are revealed below:

Stay Smart: Staying smart includes knowing what is going on in the market, knowing the properties that are vacant, and those that are not. Staying smart does not apply to you only, but also to your real estate agent. He or she needs to give you updates on the market. As soon as a house is newly listed for sale, be the first to make an offer.

Make your best offer: More of this is explained in this chapter as you keep reading. Do not beat around the bush; know how to give the right price while making your offer. To make things easier, you can attach a letter stating the reasons why you are interested in the property. Offer the best price you can.

Know Your Seller: Knowing sellers means knowing the reasons why they want to sell their properties. This will help you to know how to make your offer smartly.

Offer to clean it up: You can look like the perfect buyer to your seller if you do something unique to the property even before closing the offer. You can offer to get rid of that long-term junk in or around the house. This makes your seller happy; it makes your seller see how serious you are about making the property yours.

The Escalation Clause: When you notice you are not the only one making an offer on a property, you can make use of the escalation clause. The escalation clause should only be used in real estate contracts when there are multiple offers. You can submit your offer agreeing to add a specific amount to whatever any other person giving a higher price than yours is offering.

Close quickly: Sellers love buyers that make promises and keep those promises on time. It is better to avoid giving a longer closing date; therefore, give a shorter date and keep to it.

Do not give up: If you are really interested in a property, do not relax because your offer on a property was turned down. Be persistent; include more with your next offer. You may end up getting what you want.

The Offered Price

Some rental property investors find this part a very big deal when making their offer. Despite the fact that these investors know how much the property is worth, they still make the mistake of offering a price when they do not know the exact price to pay. Some are even confused when they offer the same price that a seller wants to sell their property, while others do not know whether they should offer a higher price or a lower price. You could be one of them.

This part is to guide you on how to offer a price.

Whether you will be offering the exact price, a lower price, a higher price, or something in between, it all depends on how long the property has been on the market (time) and the market itself.

Time and Market

If you see a property that has been on the market for a long period of time and it appears you are most likely the only one interested in it at that moment, you can try making a lower offer; properties in this situation probably have sellers that are eager to sell as soon as possible. You can be lucky by getting your offer accepted, but be careful not to beat the price by too much and get an angry 'no' from the seller.

Making a lower offer does not depend on how beautiful or how ugly a house looks. You should not give a lower offer for a very big and/or ugly house in a competitive market; you will definitely end up getting a 'no' for a reply. To avoid getting a 'no' for that ugly 'hot cake,' you can make a higher offer, but not too high.

Being successful at making offers determines how far you will go financially in rental property investment.

Chapter 13 How To Find Real Estate Investment Properties?

he benefits of investing in real estate are overwhelming. While the stock market can swing left and right and go bust occasions, the real estate market is fairly stable. That is to say that the inherent value in a real estate property you own will still be available even when the market prices have dropped down a little bit. This makes real estate the flavor of the rich.

Why? If you don't buy an income-producing real estate, you're not going to make any money investing in real estate. A real estate can actually become a liability when it takes money out of your pocket more than it makes you. This is why you have to be careful when looking for a real estate property. You want to look for an asset that will appreciate over time and produce regular cash flow.

On the flip side, finding a real estate investment property is not easy. There's a lot of work and skills required to find a good real estate investment property. The first step is to look for many options and choose from then. Sometimes, a key way to help find good real estate investment properties is your strategy.

For instance, if your strategy involves buying, fixing, and selling properties, then what you need is to search for real estates that are not in good condition and buy them lower than their market prices. You need to have criteria or check for selecting what best fits your strategy. After you purchase the property, you simply have to fix and then sell it back to the market.

However, if your strategy involves buying and renting out, you need to have a yardstick for selecting the right real estate property. In this case, you might buy a worn our real estate, fix and rent or simply buy one with little issues and then put it back to the market place. The plan is to find a real estate property that meets your plan, objective, and investing strategy.

Where to Find Real Estate Investment Properties

If you're looking to purchase good real estate investment properties, there a couple of places you have to turn to. You need to have a clear idea of what you want so that you can easily pick out and select what fits your needs. Nonetheless, the following places can serve as a good start for finding good real estate investment properties.

Real Estate Network

The importance of building your network cannot be underestimated. Your network can be a valuable source of assistance when you are looking to buy real estate. You see, building your network is more like signing up for an insurance policy and paying your monthly premiums. You never know when disaster will strike. You just keep paying your premium until one day when an accident happens.

At that time, you simply call your insurance broker to process a claim for your issue. Since you've been faithful in keeping the terms of the policy, the insurance company will take care of all the charges related to the accident that has happened. In that way, the insurance premium will actually pay off. That's the same way building a network works in real estate.

You need to be active and be intentional in building your network. If you're in the game of real estate, it is very important that you build a strong relationship network. It's through your relationship that you will be able to get some of the most prestigious and profitable real estate properties. The network you will build today will work for you in building your net worth tomorrow.

So, what do you do to build your network? Here're a few suggestions:

- Join a real estate owner's association in your city/town or community.
- Join real estate investment clubs in your city/town/community.
- Make friends with other real estate investors in your city/town/community.
- Attend real estate investing conferences/seminars and workshops.
- Reach out to help other real estate investors in one way or another.
- Build a relationship with professionals such as realtors accountants, attorneys, realtors that work for real estate owners/investors.
- Build a good relationship with bankers that deal with real estate related activities.
- Contact property managers in your city/town or community and tell them of your needs.
- Make friends with politicians and city officials that deal with the selling of real estate properties
- Let your family, relatives, and friends know that you're into real estate investing.

- Let your church or any social association you belong to know that you're into real estate investing.
- Provide social responsibility to your community under the name of your real estate company.
- Join meetups and online groups that deal with real estate investing activities.

There's no one single way to building your network, and you can't say that you've got enough network, so there's no need to keep building it. No! You have to understand that some of the opportunities you need tomorrow will be catered for by the network you have today. You have to constantly be building your network for the future. That's the key to success in real estate investing.

Real Estate Brokers/Agent

You need to see real estate brokers/agents as your eyes in the market. When you have good brokers, they will make you money by bringing you good real estate properties with incredible financing opportunities that will make you successful in the long run. A good broker should be more like an advisor, counselor and guide to buying high-quality real estate properties.

Many solo real estate investors want to do it all by themselves. Therefore, they don't see the need to buy real estate properties. They think that using a broker or agent to buy a real estate property will be a lot of hassle. They want to save money by doing the job of searching for the real estate market. Thus, they are not able to scale their real estate investment portfolio.

Even if you're the solo type, you have to learn to leverage real estate brokers and agents to find good real estate properties. You see, successful real estate investors don't become successful because they want to micromanage every step of their real estate investment. They leverage brokers and agents to help them find good real estate, and that saves them time to do other things.

Instead of using all your time to actively search for properties, you can leverage the expertise of a real estate broker who is always in the market. A real estate broker has a wealth of experience, understanding, and knowledge about the real estate market. They know the prices of real estate and how to process all the buying arrangements. With their support and guidance, you can buy good properties.

The challenge is finding good real estate agents/brokers. They are some real estate brokers who are just there to make money for themselves. They sell your property without looking at the financials and the economics of the property. That's why you need to put in enough time into selecting and choosing the right broker. If you have a good broker, everything will seem easy!

So, how do you find a good broker?

- Ask your network for recommendation
- Check their track records and accomplishments
- Focus on their integrity more than their credentials
- Check whether the realtor offers the kind of property you need.
- Ensure that you and the realtor are at the same pace when it comes to money.
- Interview as many real estate agents as possible and select the one which best fits you.
- Look for testimonials and other information provided by real estate investors.

With the help of a good real estate broker, you can be able to get an elite property that will multiply your network over a short period of time. Your real estate broker will work as your partner and help find properties that meet your investing strategies and objectives.

Real Estate Websites

If you're looking for real estate properties, the opportunities are boundless. Day in day out, many property owners want to sell their estates and make money. There are some people who have inherited properties that they want to sell out. For some people, their job demands to move to another country and work, meaning they have to sell their current property. Divorce and separation also lead to the selling of some vital and valuable real estate properties.

Many of these people get overwhelmed by their situation. They are usually individual real estate owners who are looking to sell their properties and move on to the next phase of life. Most of them don't even know what to do or how to go about selling their real estate properties. To make things simple and easy, they use real estate websites to look for potential buyers.

The real estate websites might decide to charge them something small for listing or selling their property through their platform. This is often to weed out scammers who might be using the site for their dubious activities. The real estate websites will often provide detailed descriptions about the property. Among others, the following information will be provided: the price, cap rate, neighborhood, location, size of the property, current status of the property, and many more.

Some of the most popular websites known for making real estate listing include the following:

- Craigslist.org: They help you to place bids for real estate in a certain location and also look for real estate properties that have been placed by real estate owners and realtors.
- Auction.com: They deal with all kinds of bidding related to residential properties. If you're looking to buy houses, fix them up and rent to the market, looking through this place is really great.
- Trulia App: This is simply an app that gets you closer to the market and helps you to find local real estate properties that have been listed by their individual owners in your local area. You can download this app from Google Play Store or Apple Store.
- Loop Net: If you're focused on looking for commercial properties to boost your real

estate portfolio, regularly checking and placing bids on this site is very important.
- Local Websites: Look for local community based real estate websites in your area. These websites provide a listing of local properties, and you can be able to find the property that best fits your needs in the right area or locality.

Searching for properties on the real estate website is not a one-way affair. You need to be focused and consistent in searching to find something good. Just placing your bid on the website and then waiting for miracles to happen will not happen. You have to consider following up since other real estate investors might also be looking at the property. Use contact numbers that will make it easy for sellers to reach or get to you.

You need to be careful when looking for deals through any property. Just because something looks good online does not mean you should make buy it. Before you buy any property that has been listed on any real estate website, ensure you have investigated and looked at the property carefully. Inspect the team with a qualified real estate inspection team. Save yourself a lot of hassle by doing the due diligence.

Real Estate Platforms

The internet is replete with countless opportunities to get what you want. Literally speaking, you can leverage online platforms like Google, Forums, and Groups to find good real estate properties. The idea here is to advertise. Instead of going out there to do the work of searching, you can pay some few dollars for online advertising platforms to get the job done for you.

While Facebook and LinkedIn are good social media platforms, they are not ideal for looking for real estate properties. What you want to do is to make sure you leverage digital platforms that have a high sensitivity for real estate, and you might easily get a deal there. These platforms have a lot of people looking to sell or buy real estate properties.

You need to first of all advertising in real estate forums. Look for local real estate forums with buyers and sellers. Some of these platforms place ads in their columns, which someone might see and react to. In some cases, you might not even place an ad that you want to buy a house or ant property. The buyers will themselves place ads on the platform which you can quickly respond to and buy the property.

While Google might not be your typical real estate platform, you can use it to buy properties. First of all, you can use the search bar to look for houses in any particular area. For instance, if you're looking for a house in Costa Rica, you can simply type "Single-family homes in Costarica for sale." You'll find a lot of search results from which you can look at.

Apart from using the search bar, you can place Google Ads. Using Pay-Per-Click Ads, you can be able to find a lot of people contact you for houses they are selling. This will make the job of searching very easy and fun. You simply have to go and look at what they are offering and see whether it meets your needs and criteria.

If you have a friend who has an email list of real estate audience, you consider leveraging that too. If he or she has a database of 1,000 real estate audience, and an email has been fired to them about buying any specific real estate that they might want to sell, you can be shocked at the response you will get. While this might be unusual, the deals you will get will not be available in the market. You might get better real estate deals, which will enhance your portfolio.

Real Estate Neighborhood Hunt

One of the most overlooked ways to find real estate properties is to take a jog, walk, or ride in the community you might be looking to buy a real estate property. If you want to buy a good real estate, you need to have a fair idea of how the community looks like. If you walk through the community regularly, you can instinctively know whether the community is a good fit for your real estate investment.

While you walk through the community, you can look at other properties there and figure out how they are priced, sold, and rented. By doing so, you can also find real estate properties that are for sale by their owners. This strategy has helped many real estate investors to find better deals which have not even be put in the market yet.

You need to spend some time driving through the neighborhood slowly and frequently. As you drive through the neighborhood, you need to pay attention and be hungry, looking for real estate deals that might be available. Your only cost will be your gas and time, but it will be worth it, even if you have not found any kind of property you're looking for. The lessons and things you see will trigger something and cause you to find properties in the market.

Which kind of properties should you be looking for as you drive through the neighborhood? You look for distressed properties, neglected properties, properties with for sale signs, troubled rental properties, and poorly managed real estates. With good management skills, you can buy these properties at a lower rate and then rent it or sell at a higher rate to the market.

Real Estate Magazines & Newspapers

If you're a real estate investor, then subscribing to local newspapers and magazines that deal with the real state is crucial. Instead of reading through magazines and newspapers that are not related to what you are doing, you can consider spending time and money on what will help you achieve your goals. Some of these magazines/newspapers provide deals that you'll be shocked at.

Instead of just skimming through the magazine or newspaper, consider checking the real estate column and look at the deals that are available. Read through the descriptions provide and look at other related properties therein. You should not be in haste when looking at these properties. And don't just believe it because it's in the papers.

You should make a habit of reading through the real estate properties in the newspapers and magazines from time to time. Contact their respective owners and ask for an appointment to look at the underlying property. As usual, you should ensure that you are inspecting the property with a qualified team. This will ensure that you look at the details surrounding the property.

Use Multiple Ways

There's no single way. What you have to do is to use all the steps provided. You never know which will work. Build your network, get in touch with a good real estate broker/agent, find deals on real estate websites, place bids on online platforms, and drive through the neighborhood.

By being consistent and steady in your search, you will food a good real estate property that will fetch you a robust cash flow over a period of time.

Conclusion

Rental property business is a profitable one for those who are ready to take the bull by the horns. The rental property industry is a very competitive one that has been existing for so many years since property owners realized the income they could generate from renting or leasing their buildings or land to tenants.

You can only own or manage a rental property by purchasing one. Purchasing real estate is the first step in becoming a real estate owner. It is not just owning or managing a rental property that matters but being successful in your rental property career. If you want to be successful in the rental business industry, you need to understand the rudiments of managing rental properties.

Maintenance is very important when it comes to property management; it is one of the key factors in managing rental property. There are other aspects of rental property management; they include tenant management, financial management, fulfilling your financial obligations as a rental owner, ensuring the safety and security of your tenants, and working with team members.

Creating a good relationship with your tenants is key to being a successful property owner or manager. If you own or manage a rental property, you need to understand that you will be dealing with people, and you will have employees and contractors that work with you. A huge chunk of managing a rental property involves people.

Managing rental property is not for those who are not ready to give all it takes. Before venturing into the rental property business, you need to know if you have got what it takes to manage a rental property properly. Managing a rental property is a daunting task and yet a very profitable and interesting job if you know the right things to do.

Being a successful rental owner or manager involves knowing what rental property management is all about. Having discussed important topics and steps in managing your rental property in this book, you can stay at the top of your rental property business.

At this point, you can agree that the concept of real estate is a fascinating one with lots of interesting twists that only gets better with the more knowledge you continue to acquire. Investing in real estate is a very lucrative business avenue that can bring in substantial profits. But you have to play the cards right, or else, the profitable tables can turn and become a disaster in your face. The information needed is interesting, not hidden, as long as you look in the right places. This book is a practical book that has been able to give a concise but equally informative basis on what anyone will need to thrive in the real estate industry. The principles that guide real estate investments aren't very technical that they cannot be understood by any investor. As long as you have the right team around and you make the best inquiries together with being open-minded, you have a very high chance of making the best out of every opportunity.

This book has covered every necessary aspect of real estate. At first, you got a brief introduction to real estate and background to its history. Then, the benefits of real estate were examined together with the reason why the industry is in vogue in terms of investment at the moment, and the many benefits you stand to gain from indulging it. We went further to discuss the different types of real estate that exist, the types of income you can acquire from them, and the strategies you can indulge in making them work. The three major forms of real estate (wholesales, lease options, and foreclosures) were assigned individual chapters to fully explain what they entail and why you should indulge them in suiting different purposes. You're introduced to the concept of true market value, the comparable approach, and why there's a need to segment market areas. Another very important aspect that wasn't left out is the need to put together the right team and the professionals that need to be there. Locating and targeting motivated sellers who are the best kinds of buyers for every real estate deal was also stressed. Because the key to a good investment is buying right, you'll have to go the extra mile to find these people that'll sell rightly to you. The fact that one of the major reasons why people aren't encouraged to enter into real estate deals is because of a lack of funds or knowledge to go about this. Perhaps this was you at the beginning of the book. You've made to realize that the best way to get financing is to get creative and try solving the problems of the seller. There was so much emphasis on seller financing as the best form of investment financing. The best ways to begin, negotiate, and close deals were also detailed. The book finally closed with the ways to make offers to the property owners and enter into a proper contract.

So what's next now that you've been introduced to and now know the effective strategies that work for real estate investment? We're assuming that the reason you picked up this book in the first place was to get adequate knowledge on real estate because it's either you're already in it, or you're about to, or you're just interested in it. Whatever category you fall into, your interest in investing in this area has definitely gone higher. Now, you're equipped to start investing. Some of the chapters in this book have an activity log that gives a to-do list for every reader to follow through to get an understanding of the chapter. As a matter of fact, it's advisable that you go over and over the book as many times as you can to be sure you don't leave any aspect out. Pick up a journal and mark out the plan you have chosen to follow. If it's wholesale deals, you can find your way through. For foreclosure and lease options also, virtually everything you'll need is indicated in the book.

Another important thing you should never forget with real estate investment is that you always have to be in the loop. The market is largely affected by the current economic situation in your country and vicinity. You don't only have to be up-to-date in real estate news, but also have little information about what's happening amongst the mortgage brokers and bankers, what's new in the legal aspect of real estate, what tax policies you can take advantage of to aid your investment financing and a whole lot more. The real estate market is also an ever-evolving one. The things that are working right today may be obsolete in the next ten to twenty years, or even closer than that.

You have to remain flexible also to survive in the field. Agility and being on your feet has to be something you can do effortlessly. Although technology has made a whole lot easier together with the fact that you're working with other professionals, there're still a few steps you'll have to take on your own.

It may be true that real estate investment is a great avenue to achieve your financial goals; it isn't riches that'll come to you while you're not putting in a reasonable amount of effort. It really isn't for the faint at heart or those who seek quick riches. But following through with its principles with diligence brings great reward. After putting in the necessary efforts, you can sit back and see your investments reel in sustainable wealth that can, that will leave a good mark on your financial stance.

CPSIA information can be obtained
at www.ICGtesting.com
Printed in the USA
LVHW052014131220
674086LV00033B/1202